BOXING

BY

EDWIN L. HAISLET

Assistant Professor of Physical Education
Boxing Coach, University of Minnesota
Director, Northwest Golden Glove

PUBLISHED BY
JOHN R. ORMSBY, JR.
for
BEMJO MARTIAL ARTS LIBRARY

Library of Congress Catalog Number 82-81591

ISBN 0-943736-00-5

**PUBLISHED BY
JOHN R. ORMSBY, JR.
for
BEMJO MARTIAL ARTS LIBRARY**

PREFACE

THIS BOOK is the outgrowth of sixteen years' close association with boxing. It is the answer to the evident need for a book which would present simply, concisely, and graphically the technique of boxing. Boxing is mainly in the field of motor learning, which means habit formation and the development of skill. It is important then that each skill receives the proper emphasis at the right time. Incorrect method, together with improper teaching sequence, especially when hierarchies of skill must be developed, definitely limit the possibilities of learning. The automatization of skills and elements of skills in their proper sequence is absolutely essential to the greatest ultimate development.

The problem in boxing is not only which skills and techniques to learn, but when and how to learn them. Literature in the field at the present time seemingly ignores this problem. In any field where continued development rests upon the mastery of each element in its correct place, the learning sequence is all important. Great skill in boxing can result only through mastery of each technique in its proper place. There is a proper learning sequence in boxing which, if followed, allows a natural development to result. Ignore it and the development of skill is definitely limited.

The learning sequence herein presented is the result of experiment and experience. It is not perfect and no doubt further experience will bring constructive changes. It is, however, a sequence which seems to bring the quickest results and greatest skill with a minimum output of time and energy. Followed closely, it enables the student of boxing to continue as far as is desired, ability and determination being the only limiting factors.

Acknowledgment is made to my wife, Mary Margaret, for the technical editing of this book, and to Phil Brain of the University of Minnesota for the photographs upon which the drawings are based.

CONTENTS

CHAPTER I

THE FUNDAMENTAL POSITION

DEFINITION

THE FUNDAMENTAL boxing position is that position most favorable to the mechanical execution of the techniques and skills which make up boxing. It allows complete relaxation yet at the same time gives a muscle tonus most favorable to quick reaction time. It helps to coördinate hands and feet so that maximum speed and efficiency will result, which in turn permits the greatest possibilities for either attack or defense. It insures that the feet are always under the body and therefore that the body is always in balance.

EXPLANATION

A square stance was used during the Grecian period, that is, the left arm was folded high and close to the body and used primarily for defensive purposes while the right arm was used in a hooking, swinging movement.

In England the boxing position seems to have developed from the fencing position, with the right foot and hand carried forward, with the left side of the body back.[1] As the desire developed to hit with both hands, the square and then gradually the present so-called orthodox stance evolved. Clarke [2] suggests the reason to be that the left hand was found to be faster than the right hand from the square stance.

There is little doubt that the present orthodox position resulted because of right-handed hitting. For any movement of the right hand in which power is needed, it is only natural to stand with the left foot forward. It is the natural movement in all throwing events, and it is the position of the blacksmith when swinging a sledge. Because most people are right-handed, it is necessary to shift the left foot forward in order to obtain power in right-handed blows.

[1] Norman Clarke, *How to Box*. New York: Doran and Company, 1925, p. 42.
[2] *Loc. cit.*

USE

The primary purpose of boxing is hitting. Therefore, the use of the fundamental position is to obtain the most favorable position for hitting. To hit effectively it is necessary to shift the weight constantly from one leg to the other. This means perfect control of body balance. Balance is the most important consideration of the fundamental position.

Balance is achieved only through correct body alignment. The feet, the legs, the trunk, the head are all important in creating and maintaining a balanced position. The arms are important only because they are the vehicles of body force. They only give expression to body force when the body is in proper alignment. A position of the hands and arms which facilitates easy body expression is important. The foot position is the most important phase of balance. Keeping the feet in proper relation to each other as well as to the body helps to maintain correct body alignment.

Too wide a stance prevents proper body alignment, destroying balance but obtaining solidity and power at the cost of speed and efficient movement. A short stance prevents balance as it does not give a basis from which to work. Speed results but at a loss of power and balance.

The secret of the proper stance is to keep the feet always directly under the body which means that the feet should be a medium distance apart. Either the weight is balanced over both legs or the weight is carried slightly forward over a straight left leg with the left side of the body forming a straight line from the left heel to the tip of the left shoulder. This position permits relaxation, speed, balance, and easy movement as well as a mechanical advantage, making possible tremendous power.

THE TECHNIQUE OF THE FUNDAMENTAL POSITION

THE FEET

From a natural standing position shift the weight directly over the right leg until the right side of the body forms a straight line; then raise the left foot slightly off the floor. Rotate the whole left leg inward, and place the left foot on the floor with the left toe touching the toe of the right foot on about a forty-degree angle (Figure 1, page 3). Without altering the relative foot positions, take one step forward with the left foot, shifting the weight to the left leg. The left foot is now flat on the floor, rotated inward on about a forty-degree angle. The left leg and left side of the body should form a straight line, although the left knee is loose and easy, neither locked nor bent. As the weight is shifted

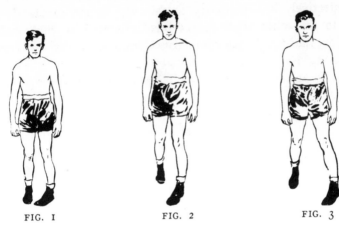

FIG. 1   FIG. 2   FIG. 3

The Fundamental Stance

to the left leg, the right heel raises off the floor and the right knee is bent with the toe of the right foot pointing directly forward (Figure 2, page 3).

This position may be too narrow. Therefore, to make a wider base, move the right foot three or four inches to the right making sure that

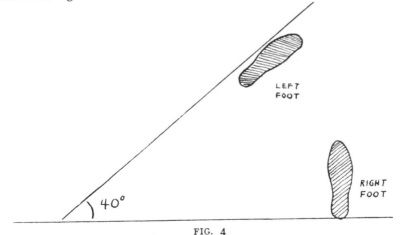

FIG. 4

Diagram of Proper Foot Position

the foot is moved directly to the right and not backward (Figures 3 and 4, page 3). Thus a wide base is obtained without sacrificing speed or power.

THE TRUNK

The position of the trunk is controlled primarily by the position of the left foot and leg. If the left foot and leg is in the correct position, the trunk automatically assumes the proper position. The one important thing about the trunk is that it should form a straight line with the left leg (Figure 5).

FIG. 5

The Fundamental Position

As the left foot and leg is turned inward, the body rotates to the right, which presents a narrow target to the opponent. If, however, the left foot and leg is rotated outward, the body is squared toward the opponent presenting a large target. For defensive purposes the narrow target is advantageous, while the square position lends itself better to attack.

THE LEFT ARM AND HAND

Hold the left arm in a folded position, elbow down and in front of the short ribs. Carry the left hand about shoulder height and off the left shoulder to the left as far as possible without raising the left elbow. Place the left hand forward eight to ten inches from the left shoulder, the arm relaxed and easy, at rest because of the proximity of the triceps to the latissimus muscle. Turn the hand so that the thumb side is up, knuckles toward the outside, the hand relaxed and open (Figure 5, page 4).

THE RIGHT ARM AND HAND

Place the right elbow directly down and in front of the short ribs, holding the right hand open with palm toward the opponent and directly in front of the right shoulder. Keep the right hand forward in line with the *left* shoulder. The arm should be relaxed and easy, ready to attack or defend (Figure 5, page 4).

THE HEAD

In boxing, the head is treated as if it were a part of the trunk with no independent action of its own. It should be carried forward, with the chin pinned down to the breast-bone. This position must never vary no matter how the body shifts. If the body turns, the head turns.

The chin is not "tucked" behind the left shoulder except in an extreme defensive position. "Tucking" the chin into the left shoulder turns the neck into an unnatural position, takes away the support of the muscles, and prevents straight bone alignment. It also tenses the left shoulder and arm, preventing free action and causing fatigue.

With the chin dropped directly forward and pinned tight to the breast-bone the muscles and bone structure are in the best possible alignment, and only the top of the head is presented to the opponent making it impossible to hit a man on the point of the chin (Figure 5, page 4).

THE UNORTHODOX POSITION

The left-handed boxer, a "southpaw" in the parlance of the ring, should take the exact opposite of the orthodox position described above. Hold the right hand and right foot forward. Do not try to change to the orthodox position until this unorthodox style is mastered. Then it is advisable to learn the orthodox form so that eventually both positions can be used.

FUNDAMENTALS OF FORM

1. The left foot is flat on the floor and turned in at an angle of forty degrees.
2. The left leg is straight but the knee is not locked.
3. The right heel is raised about two inches off the floor, with the right knee bent.

4. Weight is either balanced between both legs or shifted slightly to the front leg.
5. The left side of the body forms a straight line with the left leg.
6. Both elbows are carried down and in front of the short ribs.
7. The left hand is carried down almost shoulder height, eight to ten inches in front of the body, and to the left as far as possible without raising the left elbow.
8. The right hand is carried up, palm open toward the opponent, and directly in front of the right shoulder.
9. The chin is dropped forward to the breast-bone and tightly pinned.

CHAPTER II

THE ART OF HITTING

DEFINITION

THE ART OF HITTING is the art of obtaining maximum power in blows with a minimum of effort. Because boxing is a sport in which one contestant attempts to outhit the other by means of well-timed and maneuvered blows, hitting is the foundation of boxing.

EXPLANATION

Hitting is truly an art for it is the systematic study of how to hit straight and fast most effectively while using body power rather than mere arm power.

The ability to hit straight from the shoulder is not a natural act. It cannot be learned by chance and experience does not teach it. Straight hitting, with body power behind each blow, is an art that takes years of study and practice to perfect.

The records of history tell us that early boxing was done almost entirely with the bent arm, that is, by swinging and hooking. Such a method seems to be nature's way of hitting as evidenced from a study of wild life. Both the cat and the bear families slap and cuff. The natural tendency for an untrained person when fighting is to swing. Straight hitting, then, must be studied to be learned.

Straight hitting was established during the Golden Age of the Prize Ring, but was brought to its highest development by James J. Corbett in America. It is important because it is much faster and more accurate than curved hitting, for a straight blow will "beat" a hook or a swing in every instance. There is less chance of missing with a straight blow and because of the greater frequency of hits more damage can be done. Because balance is less disturbed, straight hitting is safer, surer, and easier.

Straight hitting is based upon an understanding of body structure and the value of leverage. It is an attempt to use body weight in every blow, hitting with the body, the arms being merely the vehicle of force. Arm action alone is insufficient to give real power to blows. Real power, quick and accurate, can be obtained only by shifting the weight in such a manner that the hip and shoulder precede the arm to the center line of the body. Otherwise, at the moment of impact there will not be full body weight behind the blow. There are only two methods which obtain a complete shift of weight. One method is a pivot or quick turn of the waist allowing the hip and shoulder to precede the arm, the other being a full body pivot, shifting the weight from one leg to the other. The waist pivot is faster and easier to learn and is used as the basis of teaching the art of hitting.

To see a boxer hit straight from the shoulder looks very simple, yet it is the most difficult technique of all boxing to learn.

Hitting does not mean pushing. True hitting may be likened to a snap of a whip—all the energy is slowly concentrated and then suddenly released with a tremendous outpouring of power. Pushing is exactly the opposite, with the concentrated force at the start of the blow and a subsequent loss of power as the arm leaves the body. In real hitting the feet are always directly under the body. In pushing, the body is often off-balance as the force of the blow does not come from a pivot of the body but from a push off the right toe.

The theory of hitting may best be grasped through analogy. Picture if you will a board, two inches by twelve inches, and two feet long. Through the center of this board is placed a rod on which the board will turn easily from side to side. Hinged to the upper two corners of the board are two small pipes. Ordinarily, the pipes would hang directly down, but instead, imagine that they are held forward at right angles to the board. Now, by turning the board on the rod one of the pipes will be forced out straight ahead, while the other pipe will recede directly backward. When the board is turned in the opposite direction, the action is reversed.

That is the correct principle of hitting. The board corresponds to the trunk of the body and the two pipes the arms. Imagine a rod placed directly through the center line of the body, that is, the spinal column. Now, turn to the left, then to the right, and as the shoulder reaches the center line of the body one arm is forcibly extended while the other arm is folded close to the body.

Power in hitting comes from a quick twist of the waist, not a swinging, swaying movement, but a pivot over the straight left leg. As long as this straight line is maintained, as long as the hips are relaxed and free to swing, as long as the shoulders are turned through to the center line of the body before the arms are extended, power will result and hitting will be an art. Once the straight line of the left side of the body is broken, power is lost because the straight left side of the body is the anchor, the pivot point, the hinge from which power and force is generated to its greatest height.

So great is the power that may be attained in this manner that a real artist in boxing can deliver a knockout blow without taking a single step forward or displaying any apparent effort.

USE

The purpose of hitting in boxing is obvious. As long as the whole idea of boxing is to hit the opponent without being hit in return, then the primary purpose of hitting is to be able to hit hard and fast and to prevent the opponent from hitting back—thus scoring points and winning the match.

THE TECHNIQUE OF HITTING

THE TURN OR PIVOT

Stand erect, feet on a line, toes forward, one natural stance apart. Arms should hang free and easy at the sides. Imagine a rod placed directly through the head, down the spine, and into the floor. A rod so placed would allow only one movement, a turning or pivoting of the body left or right. The rod would prevent swinging, swaying or bending in any direction (Figure 6, page 10).

With the body in the above position, turn left and right allowing the arms to swing. Be sure that the waist turns the arms, not that the arms turn the waist. The arms will swing out freely with every turn of the body. Bring the shoulder well around on every turn with the hips swinging freely. Continue turning from left to right until this movement is firmly established (Figures 7 and 8, page 10).

THE CLOSE-ELBOW TURN

Without altering the stance, bend the arms at the elbows, open the hands, and bring them to a position eight to ten inches directly in front of the eyes (Figure 9, page 10). The elbows are down close in front of the body, the forearms forming a straight line from the elbow to the tip of the fingers.

Now, turn the body as in the previous exercise using the waist to turn the body well through without any swinging or swaying. The turn

FIG. 6   FIG. 7   FIG. 8   FIG. 9   FIG. 10

The Body Turn or Pivot

of the body is a straight pivot. The position of the hands does not change during this movement. Keep the chin down on the breast-bone as if it were pinned there. Continue this exercise until it can be easily performed.

THE ARM EXTENSION, PALMS UP

Again assuming the above position, reach out with the left arm, palm up, to a point in front of the body which represents the median or center line. The right hand, palm up, is held on the chest, lined up directly behind the left hand, so that a straight line may be sighted between the two hands. Turn the body to the left and while turning drive the right hand to the exact spot vacated by the left (Figure 10, page 10). As the right hand drives out into extension, the left arm folds to the body, elbow down, palm in and eye level. Continue turning until the arms can be driven forward like pistons.

The principle of the rod should not be forgotten. The twist of the waist is a direct turn from right to left, with no swinging or swaying. The elbows are in, palms up and open. Each arm must be completely extended on every turn of the body. The arm must be extended on a straight line, driving slightly upward, and returned on the same straight line. In other words, the plane of the fist never varies and the elbow never drops back of the body line.

How to Make a Fist

Before attempting to hit with a closed fist, it is essential to learn how to properly clench the hand to make a fist. Improper clenching of the hand, as well as the lack of knowledge of how to use the fist for hitting purposes, accounts for most of the broken and disfigured hands.

To make a tight fist place the fingers in the center of the palm and close the thumb over and across the phalanges of the second and third fingers so that the thumb-side of the hand is perfectly flat (Figure 11, page 11).

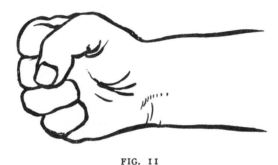

FIG. 11

The Tight Fist

Driving Both Hands Through

Now assume the fundamental position. Perform the same hitting exercise as before but with clenched fists. In the fundamental position the fist is held so that the thumb side is upward. As the body is turned to the right, and the left arm driven into extension, the wrist is turned inward, so that at the moment of impact the thumb side of the hand is in, knuckles up. This quarter turn of the wrist is a natural movement of the arm and gives a snap to the blow impossible to obtain in any other manner.

With the left arm now held out into complete extension, line the right hand up directly behind it. Quickly turn the body to the left, driving the right hand into complete extension, the left arm folding to the body, elbow down, hand up and open in position of guard (Figures 12 and 13, page 12). Continue this exercise until it becomes automatic in execu-

FIG. 12   FIG. 13

Driving Both Hands Through

tion. Remember, if the elbows are carried close, if the hands are carried high, if the plane of the fist never varies, if the body takes the elbow, if the twist of the waist furnishes the propulsion for the blow, if the principle of the rod is carefully observed, if practice is continued until skill becomes automatic, then hitting will be an art in the fullest sense.

FUNDAMENTALS OF FORM

1. Hitting is done with the body, not the arms; the arms are merely the vehicles of force.
2. Body hitting means a snap blow, not a push.
3. Power in boxing is obtained through a straight turn or twist of the waist with the shoulder and hip following through to the center line of the body.
4. The principle of the rod must be observed at all times, no swinging, no swaying, no pushing off with the right foot.
5. The left side of the body and the left leg should maintain a straight line. This is the hinge around which body weight and power rotates.
6. Arm extension takes place only after the hip and shoulder are turned through to the center line of the body.
7. The plane of the fist should never vary. In other words, drive the arm straight for a point and return it through the same plane.

8. The elbows are folded to or taken by the body. Elbows never drop backward past the medial line of the body.

9. In making a correct fist, the thumb-side of the hand is perfectly flat.

10. The hand rotates a one-quarter turn inward as the arm is extended so that at the moment of impact, knuckles are up and the thumb-side of the fist inward.

11. In teaching the hit there is a definite progression that must be followed—the principle of the turn, the close elbow turn, the arm extension, palm up, the making of a fist, and driving both hands through.

CHAPTER III

FUNDAMENTAL BLOWS AND BLOCKS

DEFINITION

FUNDAMENTAL blows are those which are delivered straight from the shoulder, using a quick twist of the waist as the propelling force.

Fundamental blocks are those defensive measures which require a minimum of skill and allow a maximum of protection.

EXPLANATION

Straight blows are the foundation of boxing skill. They developed late in history and therefore are the product of careful thought. Requiring speed and intelligence to use, they travel less distance than the round arm blows and will reach the mark first. Straight blows are more accurate than hooks and swings and allow full use of the arm's reach.

John Jackson, "the Gentleman Boxer," was the first exponent of the straight left lead.[1] However, its greatest development came at the time of Jim Corbett.

The straight right was used long before the left jab. It was undoubtedly used in some form during the days of Greece.[2] Ben Brain is supposed to have been the father of the straight right[3] (1786), although it was probably used long before his time.

USE

The Left Jab—is a "feeler." It is a light, easy blow, although it stings, jars, and annoys. As in football where the off-tackle play is the basis for a whole sequence of plays, so in boxing the left jab is the basis of all other blows. It is effective in keeping the opponent off balance and creating openings for other blows. It is a whip rather than a club.

Used correctly it is the sign of the scientific boxer, who uses strategy rather than force. It can be used for both defense and offense. It

[1] Trevor C. Wignall, *The Story of Boxing*, p. 62.
[2] K. T. Frost, "Greek Boxing," *Journal of Hellenic Studies*, p. 222.
[3] H. D. Miles, "Pugilistica,"*History of British Boxing*, p. 65.

requires skill and finesse as well as speed and deception. Its great advantage is that body balance is not disturbed. The left jab is simple in execution being merely a quarter turn of the body to the right and the extension of the left arm.

The Straight Right—is the opposite of the left jab. It is the heavy artillery. It should be used sparingly and only for apparent openings. It is delivered with a twist of the waist and a forceful extension of the right arm. At the moment of impact the weight shifts forward to the left leg which gives the power necessary for use as a finishing blow.

The secret of power in the straight right is using the left side of the body as a hinge and allowing the right side of the body to swing free. It is the same idea as in slamming a door. When Sam Langford was asked the secret of his hitting power he replied, " 'Tain't no secret, all I do is put my hips into them punches." [1]

It should be noted that the right is essentially a counter blow. It should not be led first because in so doing the whole body turns left, uncovering many vital parts which are difficult to cover. Thus, for all general purposes, it is best not to lead with the right.

The Left to the Body—is an effective blow used to bother the opponent, and to bring down the opponent's guard. While not ordinarily a hard blow, it can cause distress if driven to the solar plexus. It is important that the body follow the arm. In other words, a blow to the body is more effective and safer if the body is dropped to the level of the target.

The Right to the Body—is a power or force blow. It is used as a counter or after a preliminary feint with the left hand. As in the left jab to the body, the body follows the blow, although added force can be obtained by a body pivot to a position over the left foot. It is effective in pulling down an opponent's guard and can be used with great success against the tall boxer.

THE TECHNIQUE OF THE FUNDAMENTAL BLOWS AND BLOCKS

THE LEFT JAB

Here is an application of what has already been learned under the art of hitting. The left jab is merely one-half of that movement, a quarter turn of the left shoulder to the right until the center line of

[1] Jack Dempsey, "How to Hit Hard," p. 59, as quoted by John Romano, et al., *How to Box and How to Train.*

the body is reached, and then the full extension of the left arm (Figures 14, 15, 16, page 16).

FIG. 14   FIG. 15   FIG. 16

The Left Jab

Remember that as the left arm extends there is a quarter turn of the fist inward, so that at the moment of complete extension, the knuckles are turned up. The arm must travel on a straight line (slightly above shoulder height) and return on a straight line assuming the fundamental position as it returns to the body. The right arm is held in the position of guard, elbow down, hand up and open, in front of the right shoulder. In all hitting, including the left jab, all force is outward from the body, the arms merely relaxing and sinking back to the body rather than being pulled back.

It should be emphasized at this point that a blow is never *hit at a mark*. It is *driven through a mark*. Follow-through is just as important in boxing as it is in any other sport and follow-through can only be obtained by punching through and beyond the point of attack.

The jab should be a light, easy movement. Carry the shoulder and arm relaxed and ready at all times. Continue the jab until it is a natural movement. It requires long diligent practice to make the movement automatic, and to obtain speed and power without apparent effort. Accuracy should be the main objective.

BLOCKS FOR THE LEFT JAB

Two simple blocks should be learned at this time:

The catch—As a boxer leads a slow left jab to the opponent's right ear, the lead should be caught in the palm of the open right glove and forced up and out to the right. This leaves the defendant on the inside guard position and ready to carry the attack (Figure 17, page 17).

FIG. 17. *The Catch*   FIG. 18. *The Parry*

Blocks for the Left Jab

It is important that the right glove be kept open and relaxed and that the blow is caught on the lower part or butt of the hand. The movement must be kept close to the body at all times. Do not reach out to catch the opponent's blows as openings are thus created for a counter attack.

The parry—The simplest defense against a left jab is the parry, which forces an opponent's left lead across the body to the left with the right hand. The movement is light and easy. Force is not required.

As the opponent leads a left jab, flick the right hand across the opponent's approaching wrist, thus forcing the blow to the left and leaving the opponent's left side of the body exposed (Figure 18, page 17).

This movement is mainly of the wrist and hand as an arm movement is too slow and heavy. The right hand, moving inward from the point of the elbow, flicks across swiftly, as if brushing a fly away from the nose. Speed is essential. The right hand should strike the opponent's lead on the cuff of the glove or on the wrist. The right elbow must remain stationary if the movement is to be performed correctly.

THE STRAIGHT RIGHT

Of all boxing technique, the straight right is one of the most easily learned and executed blows. However, it is often difficult for the student to grasp because the fundamental principle is misunderstood.

In any power or force blow the bone structure must be aligned so as to form one straight body side or line which enables the bone structure to support the weight of the body, thus freeing the muscles to propel the other side of the body forward and creating terrific force.

One side of the body must always form a straight line. This is accomplished by merely shifting body weight over a straight leg, hinging one side of the body, and freeing the other side for a forceful turn or pivot. If power is desired in a right-hand blow, the weight must be shifted to a straight left leg in order that the right side of the body may swing forward. If power is required in a left hook, it is obtained by shifting the weight over a straight right leg and swinging the left side of the body around to the right.

The technique of the straight right is just this: Assume the fundamental position. Shift the weight forward until it is directly over the left leg (Figure 19, page 19). This allows the bones of the left side of the body to form a straight line, and all muscular power used to turn the body in order to create force. Turn the right hip and shoulder through to the center line * (Figure 20, page 19), and drive the right hand into complete extension (Figure 21, page 19).

The fist drives out at shoulder height and at the moment of impact the knuckles are turned up. The arm then relaxes back to the funda-

* The continued reference to the center line means the center or median line of the body. Such a line is the same as the sternum, or nose. The theory behind punching from the center line of the body to the point of attack is that a straight line is the shortest distance between two points. It is the fastest and most effective blow that can be used. It is the only true straight blow. Many boxers "thumb their noses" and "sniff" without knowing the reason for so doing.

FIG. 19   FIG. 20   FIG. 21

The Straight Right

mental position. The propulsion of the blow comes from the twist of the waist. As the right arm is extended, the left arm is held close to the left side, in the position of guard. This movement must be practiced until it can be easily, quickly, and correctly performed. The arm should drive out with such force as would seem to pull it clear of the socket. Again, the blow must be driven *through* and not just *at* an object.

THE GUARDS FOR THE RIGHT-HAND BLOWS

The guards for a right hook and swing are herein given together with the guards for a straight right. The beginner will frequently meet different types of right-hands, and it is essential that a defense be taught for all types from the very first.

The leverage guard—Assume the fundamental position. As the opponent leads a straight right, straighten the left arm by flinging it forcibly up and to the left. This will cause the arm to cross the path of the opponent's lead from the inside and deflect it to the outside, thus accomplishing the desired results (Figure 22, page 20).

To be successful the arm must be completely straightened, and the elbow locked at the instant of contact with opponent's lead. It is best to start the left hand slightly lower than ordinarily in order to be sure of obtaining the inside position. Force is needed in order to make the guard effective, so that the opponent's blow will not carry through. The right arm is held open and ready to guard or attack.

The shoulder block—Assume the fundamental position. As the opponent leads a straight right to the chin, turn the body to the right in order to intercept the blow on the left deltoid or shoulder muscle. At the same time tip the left shoulder upward by shifting the body weight back to the right leg. The left arm drops to a position almost alongside the left leg. The right hand is carried open and directly off the left shoulder (Figure 23, page 20).

FIG. 22. *The Leverage Guard*   FIG. 23. *The Shoulder Block*

FIG. 24. *The Drop-away*
Blocks for Right Handed Blows

The drop-away—is a form of ducking used to get away from an overhand right. Assume the fundamental position. As the opponent lunges and swings an overhand right, drop out of the range of the arc of the blow by quickly dropping the body from the waist to a position directly over the bent right leg. The weight is shifted to the right leg and the body is turned almost to the side. The left hand is dropped low protecting the left side, while the right hand is carried high ready for a left hook (Figure 24, page 20).

FIG. 25. *The Stop*   FIG. 26. *The Cross Parry*

Blocks for Right-Handed Blows

The stop—is a form of defense in which a blow is stopped before it is started. In this particular case it is used as a defense against a right hook.

Assume the fundamental position. As the opponent raises the right elbow preparatory to delivering a right hook, drive the left hand into complete extension. It is the same movement as the jab except that the left hand is held open and placed either around the opponent's biceps, or driven to the opponent's shoulder (Figure 25, page 21).

In either case it is an effective defense. When driven to the biceps it so bruises and batters the flesh that it completely disables the right arm in a short time. Driving the open left arm like a *ramrod* to the opponent's shoulder will spin him off balance rendering the hook ineffective and creating an opening for a counter attack.

The cross parry—In the parlance of the ring, this is a "sucker" guard. It requires a nicety of coördination and a finesse and precision that is found only in the most skillful boxers. Assume the fundamental position. As the opponent leads a straight right, reach over with the right hand and brush the lead to the left, thus forcing it outside and wide of its mark. This should be a light and easy movement, more wrist than arm. The elbow moves only slightly but is not raised. The left hand is lowered in order that it will not interfere with the cross parry (Figure 26, page 21).

The "sucker" part or deception is this: As the cross parry is performed, the chin is seemingly exposed to the opponent's left hook. If the opponent starts to take this advantage, merely drop the head into the crook of the right arm thus ducking under his hook, and at the same time hook the left hand to opponent's midsection.

THE LEFT JAB TO THE BODY

If the principle is followed that the body must follow the arm at all times, no difficulty will be encountered in executing the straight blows to the body.

Assume the fundamental position. Before a jab to the body can be executed, the body must be on the same level as the mark [1] in order that the blow will be straight. Therefore, drop the body forward from the waist to a position at right angles to the legs. Keep the left leg only slightly bent but the right leg more completely flexed. As the body drops, drive the left arm into forceful extension toward the opponent's solar plexus. The blow is slightly upward, never downward. The right hand is carried high in front of the body ready for the opponent's left hook. Hold the head down so that only the top of the head is visible, which will be protected by the extended left arm (Figure 27, page 23). The head should be held tight to the left arm.

THE STRAIGHT RIGHT TO THE BODY

Assume the fundamental position. Drop the body forward from the waist to a position almost at right angles to the legs and while so doing, turn to the left so that the right hip is carried forward to the center line of the body, and the right shoulder is on a line directly above the left foot. When this position is reached, drive the right arm into forceful extension. The left hand is up and open, elbow down,

[1] The "mark" is the boxing term used to designate the solar plexus.

guarding against the opponent's right hand. The head is down along the right arm and thus well protected (Figure 28, page 23).

FIG. 27. *Left Jab to Body*

FIG. 28. *Straight Right to Body*

Straight Blows to the Body

THE BLOCKS FOR THE STRAIGHT BLOWS TO THE BODY

The Step-Away—is a defensive measure whereby the point of attack is drawn out of range.

Assume the fundamental position. As the opponent leads a blow to the body (either a right- or left-hand blow) extend the left arm to the top of the opponent's head, and at the same time slide the left foot back to the right foot, the weight shifting entirely to the left foot, allowing the right foot to swing free. This movement tilts the pelvis, contracts the abdominal muscles, and brings the body out of the range of attack. The right hand should be carried high and ready for attack or defense (Figure 29, page 24).

The Elbow block—Assume the fundamental position. As the opponent leads a straight blow to the body merely turn the body so that the blow is taken on an elbow. The elbow and body are turned as one (Figure 30, page 24). Ordinarily, it is best to have the right elbow block a left lead, and the left elbow block a right lead. However, the opposite elbow may be used. The hands should not drop but should maintain their fundamental position.

FIG. 29. *The Step-away*

FIG. 30. *The Elbow Block*

FIG. 32. *The Brush-away*

FIG. 31. *The Fore-arm Block*

Blocks for Straight Blows to the Body

The forearm block—This is a dangerous block and should not be used except when necessary. It is valuable for emergency use only.

Assume the fundamental position. As an opponent leads a straight blow for the body, fold the forearms across the midsection, left arm under the right, so that the abdominal region is completely covered (Figure 31, page 24). Do not forget that while the abdominal region is being protected, the chin is exposed. Be ready to fold forward under blows delivered to the chin.

The brush-away—is the safest and easiest defense against straight blows to the body.

Assume the fundamental position. As the opponent leads a straight left to the body drop the open right glove in down and across the opponent's wrist, thus brushing the blow to the outside. The elbow hardly moves. The whole movement is a circular motion inward with the right hand and forearm (Figure 32, page 24).

It is best to use a right-hand brush for a left lead and vice versa. However, a cross brush can be used to good advantage when a counter blow is planned.

FUNDAMENTALS OF FORM

THE LEFT JAB

1. Weight or balance should not be disturbed.
2. The power of the left jab comes from the quarter turn of the left shoulder to the right and the forceful extension of the left arm.
3. The arm is driven slightly upward from the shoulder and returns through the same plane.
4. At the moment of impact the knuckles are up.
5. All the force of a blow is away from the body, the arm merely relaxes back to the body.
6. Jab through a point, not at a point.
7. The right hand is held open and ready, in the position of guard.
8. The left side of the body should form a straight line throughout the maneuver.

BLOCKS FOR THE JAB

The catch
1. Must be performed close to the body.
2. Must gain the inside position.

3. The left lead should be caught in the open right glove, down toward the butt of the hand.

The parry

1. The movement is mainly of the wrist.
2. The movement must be light and easy.
3. The right elbow must not be moved.

THE STRAIGHT RIGHT TO THE CHIN

1. Body weight must be shifted directly over the straight left leg.
2. Hip and shoulder must be turned through to the center line.
3. Then the right arm is driven into complete extension.
4. At the moment of impact the knuckles are up with the thumb-side of the fist turned inward.
5. The plane of the fist does not vary. The blow is delivered on a straight line and returned on a straight line.
6. All force is away from the body. The arm relaxes back to position.
7. The left arm folds to the body in position of guard.
8. Drive the right hand *through* a "mark," not *at* one.

THE GUARDS FOR THE STRAIGHT RIGHT

The leverage guard

1. Start the left hand low.
2. Fling the left arm forcibly up and out.
3. The left arm must be completely straightened and the elbow locked at the time of contact.
4. This guard will attain the inside position.
5. Carry the right hand high and in position to guard or counter.

The shoulder block

1. Turn the body to the right so as to catch the blow high on the left deltoid.
2. Tilt the left shoulder upward by dropping the body weight back over a straight right leg.
3. The left arm drops to a position along the left leg, ready to counter.
4. The right hand is carried high and open, close to the left shoulder.

The drop-away

1. Use only against an overhand swing.
2. Merely turn and drop the body out of the arc of the swing.

3. Drop the left hand low to protect the left side and to be ready to counter.
4. Hold the right hand off the left shoulder, open and ready.

The stop
1. The movement must be performed quickly, similar to the left jab.
2. Keep the palm of the left hand open.
3. Drive the open left hand to opponent's right biceps, thumb around or,
4. Drive the hand to opponent's right shoulder.

The cross parry
1. Reach over with the right hand and force opponent's straight lead to the outside.
2. The right arm must be kept close to the body.
3. Movement is light and easy, more wrist than arm.
4. The elbow moves very little, and does not raise.
5. The chin is exposed, so be ready for opponent's left hook.

THE LEFT JAB TO THE BODY
1. Power is obtained through a body drop from the waist, to a position over the left foot.
2. The body must follow the arm.
3. The greatest part of the body drop is obtained through a bend of the right knee.
4. The left leg is kept as straight as possible.
5. The left arm is driven straight from the shoulder to the "mark," and at the moment of contact should be perfectly straight.
6. At the moment of impact the knuckles are up.
7. The right hand is held up and open, ready for a left hook.
8. The movement must be sudden and recovery immediate.
9. The left hand is not dropped but follows the body at all times.
10. The head is carried well forward and is protected by the extended left arm.

THE STRAIGHT RIGHT TO THE BODY
1. Power is obtained through a turn of the body to the left and at the same time a drop of the body forward over the left leg.

2. The body drop is attained primarily through a bend of the right knee. The left leg is held as straight as possible.
3. As the right shoulder approximates a position over the left foot, the right arm is driven into forceful extension.
4. The body follows the arm at all times.
5. The right arm is driven in a straight line from the shoulder to the "mark."
6. At the moment of impact, knuckles are up, thumb-side of the fist in.
7. The fundamental position must be resumed immediately.
8. In the recovery of the fundamental position, the arm must follow the body. The arm must not drop at any time.
9. The left arm is held in a position of guard, waiting and ready for a right counter.
10. The head is carried forward alongside the right arm.

BLOCKS FOR THE STRAIGHT BLOWS TO THE BODY

The step-away

1. Place the left hand directly on the opponent's head and push.
2. Tilt the pelvis by dropping the left foot back to the right and shifting the weight to the left foot.
3. The right leg swings free.
4. The right hand is carried high and ready for attack or defense.
5. The sidestep is easily executed following the step-away.

The elbow block

1. Don't move the elbow, but turn the body.
2. Try to intercept the blow directly on the elbow.
3. Ordinarily, use the right elbow for a left lead and vice versa.
4. The arm which is not used to block should be held ready for the counter.

The forearm block

1. Use only when necessary.
2. Fold the left arm under the right.
3. Hands should be turned in so the broad side of the forearms are rotated outward.
4. The chin is exposed, so be ready to fold under any blows so directed.

The brush-away

1. Movement is down and inward, with either hand.
2. In executing a brush, place the open hand across or around opponent's wrist.
3. Move the elbow only as much as needed.
4. Ordinarily it is best to use the right brush for left leads and vice versa.
5. Be ready to counter with the hand not used as defense.

CHAPTER IV

FUNDAMENTAL FOOTWORK

DEFINITION

FUNDAMENTAL footwork is the ability to move the body easily and efficiently so that balance will not be disturbed. It implies the ability to attack or defend at all times.

EXPLANATION

Footwork is a comparatively new development in boxing. In the early days of Greece, to dodge or move away from a blow was considered an evidence of cowardice.

In England, footwork was used very little before the time of John Jackson [1] (1768) and it was not until the beginning of the Nineteenth Century and the school of Belcher, Bendigo and Sayer that moving in the ring was used as a means of defense as well as a means of conserving energy. [2]

Footwork developed with the use of the glove because it called for speed and skill. Today, the essence of boxing is the art of moving, moving in to attack or defend, moving out to defend or "pull off" balance. The ability to move at the right time is the foundation of great skill in boxing.

Footwork means moving the body so as to be in the best position for attack or defense. It means balance—but movement and balance together. To maintain balance while constantly shifting body weight is an art few ever acquire.

Footwork does not mean leg work nor does it mean jumping around. It means moving just enough to accomplish a purpose, in order to make an opponent miss or to deliver a counter blow effectively.

If balance is to be maintained at all times, it is absolutely necessary that the feet be always directly under the body. Any movement of the feet which tends to unbalance the body must be eliminated. The

---

[1] Trevor Wignall, *The Story of Boxing*, p. 62.
[2] Edward A. Knebworth, *Boxing, a Guide to Modern Methods*, p. 47.

fundamental position is one of perfect body balance, and should always be maintained, especially as regards the feet. Wide steps or leg movements which require a constant shift of weight from one leg to the other cannot be used. During this shift of weight there is a moment when balance is precarious, and so renders attack or defense ineffective.

The greatest phase of footwork is the coördination of the hands and feet. When the feet and hands work together automatically, the art of moving is perfection itself.

There are only four moves possible in footwork—advancing, retreating, circling left, and circling right. However, there are important variations of advancing and retreating as well as the necessity of coordinating each fundamental movement with the arms.

It is well to remember that a master of footwork can move in all directions, usually in a different direction each time. Never use the same technique twice in succession. Above all things, keep moving, for a moving target is an elusive one.

USE

The Forward Shuffle—is a slow movement forward in such a manner that both feet are on the floor at all times, with the body poised for either a sudden attack or a defensive maneuver. Its primary purpose is to create openings and to draw leads.

The Backward Shuffle—is a slow movement backward in such a manner that both feet are on the floor at all times permitting balance to be maintained for attack or defense. It is used to draw leads or to draw the opponent off balance, thus creating openings.

The Quick Advance—There are times when a slow advance will not accomplish the purpose, when sudden speed and a quick advance is necessary. Thus the quick advance, which allows sudden movement forward without loss of body balance.

The Forced Retreat—Here, again, is a technique which makes possible sudden retreat when the slow shuffle backward will not suffice. It allows a sudden forceful move backward with a sureness of balance, allowing further retreat if necessary, or a stepping forward to attack if desired.

Circling to the Left—The ability to move or circle either to left or right is an extremely important part of footwork. In general, it is true that it is best to circle away from an opponent's strongest blow. In other words, circling to the left is moving away from a left hook into the opponent's right. It is essential, then, not only to know how, but when to circle.

Circling left may be used to nullify an opponent's left hook. It may be used to get into position for terrific right-handed counters, and it can be used to throw an opponent off balance. The important things to remember are not to cross the feet while circling, to move deliberately rather than wildly, and with very little motion.

Circling to the Right—is used to keep out of the range of right-hand blows and to obtain a good position for the delivery of a left hook and a left jab. It is safer but more difficult than circling to the left and therefore should be used more often.

THE TECHNIQUE OF FUNDAMENTAL FOOTWORK

THE FORWARD SHUFFLE

This is a forward advance of the body without disturbing body balance which can only be performed through a series of short steps forward. These steps must be so small that the feet are not lifted at all, but slide along the floor.

With this principle in mind, assume the fundamental position. Slide the left foot forward about two inches, followed directly by the right foot, moving it two inches forward. The knees are not kept stiff, nor are they bent, but free and loose with a slight movement at all times. Keep the left side of the body in a straight line. The left foot is flat on the floor. The toe of the right foot is placed firmly on the floor. The entire movement is shuffle-like. The feet do not leave the floor. They slide (Figures 33, 34, 35, page 33).

Keep shuffling forward until a "body feel" results. The whole body maintains the fundamental position throughout. The key is the maintenance of the fundamental position while moving slowly forward.

THE BACKWARD SHUFFLE

The principle of the backward shuffle is the same as that of the forward shuffle, that is, a slow backward movement without disturbance of the fundamental position.

Assume the fundamental position. Now slide the right foot backwards two inches, followed by the same movement with the left foot. Continue, maintaining the fundamental position at all times (Figures 36, 37, 38, page 33).

FIG. 33   FIG. 34   FIG. 35

Fundamental Footwork—the Forward Shuffle

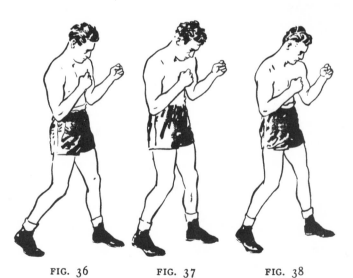

FIG. 36   FIG. 37   FIG. 38

Fundamental Footwork—the Backward Shuffle

THE QUICK ADVANCE

There are times when openings appear which only can be taken advantage of through fast movement. The ability to step in fast, with both feet under the body, gives the advantage of being able to score, and to follow up.

Assume the fundamental position. Push off smartly with the right foot, and at the same time step forward with the left foot. The left foot is carried close to the floor and the right foot is immediately brought forward so that foot positions are essentially those of the fundamental stance (Figures 39, 40, 41, page 34). The body flattens

FIG. 39   FIG. 40   FIG. 41

The Quick Advance

toward the floor rather than leaping into the air. It is not a hop. In all respects it is the same as a wide step forward—a long step with the left foot, bringing the right foot immediately into position.

THE QUICK RETREAT

This movement is essentially a long but quick step backward. Assume the fundamental position. Push off with the left foot, and at the same time step backward with the right, weight shifting to the straight right leg, using the left leg as a drag to maintain balance (Figures 42, 43, page 35).

FIG. 42   FIG. 43

The Quick Retreat

CIRCLING TO THE LEFT

In this movement the left leg becomes a movable pivot. Assume the fundamental position. Step six to eight inches to the left with the left foot. Then, using the left leg as a pivot-point, wheel the whole body to the left until the correct position is resumed. The first step with the left foot may be as short or as long as necessary, the longer the step, the greater the pivot. The fundamental position must be maintained at all times. The left hand should be carried a little higher than ordinarily in readiness for the opponent's right counter.

CIRCLING TO THE RIGHT

This is a more precise movement requiring shorter steps. Assume the fundamental position. Step from four to six inches to the right with the left foot and immediately follow with the right foot to the fundamental stance position. The step with the left foot must be short.[1] Carry the right hand high, ready for the opponent's left hook.

[1] While many instructors indicate that in circling to the right the first step should be with the right foot, experience has shown that it is best to step first with the left foot. It is faster and more natural to execute.

The Coördination of Hands and Feet

The forward and backward shuffle with the left jab

1. Assume the fundamental position. Shuffle forward slowly, jabbing out with the left hand. Jab continuously. Note that body balance is not disturbed and the rhythm of the shuffle and arm movement does not necessarily have to be the same.
2. When forward progress is stopped, shuffle backward. Jab while shuffling. Body balance should not be disturbed.

The forward and backward shuffle using the straight right

1. Assume the fundamental position. Shuffle forward slowly, driving the right arm into continuous extension. Body balance should not be disturbed.
2. When the forward progress is stopped, shuffle backward, driving the right hand into complete extension.
3. Now shuffle forward, driving first the left and then the right hand into continuous extension. The arms still work independently of the feet. Balance is not disturbed.

The quick advance and the forced retreat using the left jab

1. Assume the fundamental position. Start moving forward through a series of quick advances. As the body is moved forward each time, drive the left hand into extension, like a ramrod. The left arm works in unison with the left foot. At the instant the left foot touches the floor, the left hand is completely extended. Continue, until forward progress is impeded.
2. Then move backward through a series of forced retreats. Push off with the left foot, and jab with the left hand.
3. Same, except jab first, then push off into a forced retreat.
4. Now take one quick advance and at the same time, jab. Then take one quick retreat and jab. Make this a continuous movement, forward and back, hands and feet working together. Be sure that left arm is completely extended each time.
5. Move forward by a series of quick advances, driving the right hand into complete extension every time the right foot is moved. Carry the left hand high. Remember, the right hand and right foot move together.
6. When forward progress is impeded, move backward through a series of forced retreats, driving the right hand into complete

extension every time the right foot is moved. The foot touches the floor at the same moment the hand is completely extended. The left hand must be high and ready.

The quick advance with the left and right to the chin

1. Move forward through a succession of quick advances, the hands and feet working together. As the left step is taken, jab with the left hand. As the right foot is moved forward, drive with the right hand. Continue.

The left jab and straight right combined with circling left

1. Assume the fundamental position. Circle to the left. As the left foot is moved, jab with the left hand. Continue, left hand and foot working in unison.
2. Continue, only using the straight right. As the right foot is moved, drive the right arm into complete extension. Continue, with the right arm and right leg working as one.
3. As the left foot is moved to the left, jab with the left hand. As the right foot is moved, drive the right arm into complete extension.

The left jab and the straight right combined with circling right

1. Assume the fundamental position. Circle to the right. As the left foot is moved, jab with the left hand. Continue, left hand and left foot working together.
2. Continue, only using a straight right. As the right foot is moved, drive the right arm into complete extension. Continue, with the right hand and right foot working together.
3. Now as the left foot is moved, jab with the left hand. As the right foot is moved, pivot the body to the left and drive the right arm into complete extension.

FUNDAMENTALS OF FORM

The Forward Shuffle

1. Body weight must not be disturbed.
2. Foot movements are no more than two inches in length, the right foot following the left.
3. Both feet are on the floor at all times.
4. The fundamental position is maintained at all times.

The Backward Shuffle

1. As above, except the right foot is moved first.

The Quick Advance

1. This is really a long step forward. It is not a hop.
2. The left foot moves first, followed by the right. One foot is in contact with the floor at all times.
3. Push with the right foot and step forward with the left.
4. The right foot is brought quickly to fundamental stance position.
5. The body is flattened toward the floor.

The Quick Retreat

1. It is a sudden long step backward. The right foot moves first, followed by the left.
2. The weight is shifted to a straight right leg.
3. The left foot is used as a drag.

Circling Left

1. The left leg moves first and becomes a pivot for the body.
2. The body is now wheeled to the left, until the fundamental position is regained.
3. The left hand is held high in readiness for the opponent's right counter.

Circling Right

1. The left foot moves first, four to six inches to the right.
2. The right foot follows to position.
3. The right hand is carried high and ready for opponent's left hook.

Coördination of Hands and Feet

1. Hands and feet should work together at all times. A left-hand lead should be used only when the left foot is moved. A right-hand lead should be used only as the right foot is moved.

THE ADVANCED BLOWS AND BLOCKS

DEFINITION

ADVANCED blows are those performed with a bent arm. Advanced blocks are the defensive measures for bent-arm blows, which are most easily and efficiently performed while either guarding or blocking.

EXPLANATION

A skilled workman has a command of all the necessary knowledge and tools that the task demands. A skilled boxer has the knowledge of and the ability to perform all fundamental blows and blocks. A workman may be skilled but without the proper tools, he cannot do a good job. Neither can the boxer be successful without the tools of his trade, the fundamental skills of attack and defense.

The tool kit of the boxer must include all blows and blocks which are known and used. It is possible to execute only two types of blows—straight and bent-arm blows. The straight blows can be used to face or body with either hand. Each in itself is a complicated technique. The same is true of bent-arm blows except there are more of them—the short hook, the swing, and the uppercut. These blows, used with either hand to face or body, together with straight hitting, exhaust all the practical possibilities of hitting.[1] It follows that there is little possibility of any new blows. A slight variation in timing or combination may make the result appear to be a new blow, but actually it will be an old one in a new guise.

English stylists seldom make use of bent-arm blows. Used properly, bent-arm blows make boxing a more complete and difficult sport. Without bent-arm blows there are fewer possible combinations.

There is a reason why bent-arm blows are a part of a boxer's tool kit. Not only are they powerful counter blows, but they are one means of opening up an opponent's defense. As in football where wide sweeps and open play are used to spread the defense, in boxing constant hooking will create openings for straight blows.

[1] The one other possibility is the overhand swing or chop.

Once a boxer has mastered the hook, the swing, and the uppercut, as well as the defense for such blows, he has in combination with his straight blows all the necessary tools of his trade. He will be the journeyman who can do a good job, not yet possessing the skill, the finesse, the knowledge or the perfection of the master.

USE

The Left Hook—is used as a counter and finishing blow. It is a short blow, rarely traveling over six inches, and produces tremendous power as the whole body weight is behind it. It should be used judiciously and only when an actual opening has been created. It is used best when going in or coming out, and is useful against an overreaching left jab or swing, or a straight right or swing.

Theoretically, the hook is a head blow. The so-called body hooks are in reality uppercuts or poorly executed straight blows. The left hook is the most difficult blow in boxing to learn and use properly.

The Right Hook—is one of the most dangerous counters in boxing and is often referred to incorrectly as the "right cross." It is a finishing blow and can be used against an opponent who overreaches and is off balance. It may be used after ducking or whenever an opponent hesitates. The blow carries terrific force but should not be used too often.

The Swings to the Face or Body—are flat wide blows which carry little power. They are used mainly to widen the defense and to bother an opponent. They should be used sparingly and with caution so that the hands will not be injured.

The Short or True Uppercuts—are used principally as defensive blows against crouchers, and as counters. They are short, inside blows carrying considerable power. They are used best to the body, although they may be used occasionally to the chin. The right uppercut is more often used than the left as it is easier to execute and carries more power.

The Long Uppercuts, with Left and Right Step—These blows are extremely effective as counters against a left jab. There are two different forms of execution; first, stepping across with the left foot which gives speed at the loss of power; second, stepping with the right foot which gives power but at a loss of speed.

THE TECHNIQUE OF THE ADVANCED BLOWS AND BLOCKS

The Left Hook

Because perfect execution of the left hook calls for more coördination and precision than any other one blow, it is the most difficult blow to learn. The left hook is comprised of three movements. From the fundamental position (Figure 44, page 41).

1. Turn the left hip and shoulder to the right until a point is reached corresponding to the center line of the body. The left hand does not move with the body, but remains in the fundamental position. At the same time shift the weight over the straight right leg (Figure 45, page 41).

FIG. 44   FIG. 45   FIG. 46

The Left Hook

2. Now whip * the bent left arm in an arc to the right shoulder (Figure 46, page 41).

At the completion of the blow the weight is over the right leg, right toe pointing directly to the side, the left side of the body is turned

* The whip of the arm is caused by the turning of the body away from the arm until the range of movement in the shoulder joint is completely used. Then the arm must turn with the body. Executed quickly, this causes the arm to whip forward as if released from a bow.

toward the opponent, and the left arm is pulled across the body, the left hand approximating the right shoulder. The right arm is held inside the left arm and near the left shoulder.

THE BLOCKS FOR THE LEFT HOOK

The forearm block—Assume the fundamental position. As the opponent leads a short left hook raise the right arm as if to salute. The hand should be high and close, knuckles out, forearm straight and tight to the body, elbow down. Intercept the blow on the wrist, forearm, or elbow (Figure 47, page 42).

The inside block—Assume the fundamental position. As the opponent leads a short left hook, turn the body inward and to the left, and at the same time bend slightly forward so that the body is carried inside the opponent's hook. The right hand is carried tight and close as in a forearm block. The left hand should be placed on the opponent's right (Figure 48, page 42).

FIG. 47. *The Forearm Block*   FIG. 48. *The Inside Forearm Block*
Blocks for the Left Hook

THE RIGHT HOOK

The right hook is similar to the left hook in execution, except that it is easier.

Assume the fundamental position. Shift the weight over the straight left leg, turn the right shoulder and hip through to the center line,

From The Desk Of —

Paul Colletti

Litton
Aero Products

then raise the right elbow and in a half-bent position, whip it in an arc toward the left shoulder.

THE BLOCKS FOR THE RIGHT HOOK

The stop—is the most effective block for the right hook. For a full description turn to page 21 (Figure 25, page 21).

The shoulder catch—Assume the fundamental position. As the opponent leads a right hook, move the left shoulder forward forming a point against which the thumb of the open right glove may be hooked and then catch the blow in the open right glove.

THE LEFT SWING AND BLOCKS

The left swing—is performed exactly like the left hook except the left arm is first straightened as in a left jab, then followed by a full sweep of the arm to the right shoulder. In delivering the blow the hand is not dropped from its fundamental position. At the moment of impact the thumb-side of the hand is up and the right arm is held in the position of guard.

The blocks for a left swing—are exactly the same as those used against the left hook. If the opponent makes regular use of the left swing, counter inside with a straight right lead.

THE LEFT AND RIGHT UPPERCUTS AND BLOCKS

The left uppercut—Assume the fundamental position. Bend directly to the left and slightly forward until the left elbow is touching the left leg a few inches below the hip bone. The left arm is in a half-bent position, parallel to the floor, palm up. The right elbow is close to the side, forearm covering the right side of the body and face. Allow the left shoulder and hip to swing forward, carrying the left arm to the center line of the body. When the center line of the body is reached, straighten and whip the left arm upward in an arc for the solar plexus or the chin.

The right uppercut—Assume the fundamental position. Bend to the right and slightly forward, so that right elbow is touching the right leg below the hip, and the right arm is in a half-bent position, parallel to the floor, palm up (Figure 49, page 44). Rotate the body to the left, turning the right hip and shoulder to the center line (Figure 50, page 44), then suddenly straighten the body and whip the right hand upward to the solar plexus (Figure 51, page 44). The left arm covers the left side of the body and face throughout.

The most effective defense—for an uppercut is merely moving a few inches backward out of range. However, the brushaway, merely dropping the open glove across the opponent's wrist, is very effective. It is best to use the right brush for the left uppercut and vice versa.

FIG. 49   FIG. 50   FIG. 51

The Uppercuts

THE LONG UPPERCUT AND BLOCKS

With a left step—Assume the fundamental position. As the opponent jabs a left lead, parry to the outside position with a right hand, at the same time taking a quick step with the left foot. Drop the left arm to a position perpendicular to the floor (Figure 52, page 45). As the weight shifts to the left leg, whip the left hand upward to the opponent's abdomen (Figure 53, page 45).

With a right step—Assume the fundamental position. Using the right hand to parry opponent's left lead to the outside guard position, drop the left arm to a position perpendicular to the floor, palm upward, and step briskly one step sideward and forward with the right foot (Figure 54, page 45). As the weight shifts to the right leg, whip the left arm upward to opponent's abdomen. After the parry, the right hand is held high and off the left shoulder.

FIG. 52. *With Left Step*   FIG. 53. *The Finish*

FIG. 54. *With Right Step*
The Long Uppercuts

The most effective defense—is to merely drop an open glove in and downward across opponent's forearm, forcing the blow to the outside. It is best to use the right brush for the left uppercut and vice versa.

FUNDAMENTALS OF FORM

THE LEFT HOOK
1. Turn the left hip and shoulder through to the center line, away from the left arm which retains its original position.
2. Shift the weight back to the straight right leg.

3. Turn the body to the right and whip the left hand in an arc to the right shoulder.
4. Drive *through* the "mark," not *toward* it.
5. The left hand is not lowered or "telegraphed" in any manner.
6. Knuckles are pointing out, palm inward at the moment of impact. The thumb-side of the hand is up.
7. The right hand is carried off the left shoulder, open and in position of guard.

Blocks for the Left Hook
The forearm block
1. The movement is similar to a salute.
2. The arm must be held close and tight to the body, elbow down.
3. Chin should be well tucked.

The inside forearm block
1. Turn the body with the hook, dropping slightly forward inside the hook.
2. Keep the elbow down, forearm tight against the body.

The Right Hook
1. Shift the weight over a straight left leg.
2. Turn the right hip and shoulder through to the center line.
3. Raise the right elbow and with the arm in a half-bent position, whip it in an arc toward the right shoulder.
4. At the moment of impact, knuckles should be turned out, thumb-side of the hand up.
5. Wrist must be kept straight.
6. The left arm is held in position of guard.

The Blocks for the Right Hook
The stop
1. As the opponent raises his elbow, drive the open left hand to his biceps.
2. The arm must be completely straightened, thumb around the biceps.
3. Carry the right hand high and ready to block or counter.

The shoulder catch
1. Hunch the left shoulder forward, hooking the thumb of the right hand into crook of the shoulder.

2. Catch opponent's right hook in open right glove.
3. The left hand is lowered slightly, ready to counter over opponent's right.

THE LEFT SWING
1. The left arm should be completely extended as in a left jab.
2. Turn the left hip and body toward the opponent.
3. Shift the body weight back to the straight right leg.
4. Whip the left arm in a full arc toward the right shoulder.
5. The hand is not lowered or "telegraphed" in any way.
6. At the moment of impact the hand is turned so that the thumb-side of the hand is up.

THE LEFT AND RIGHT UPPERCUTS
1. Bend the body slightly forward and directly to the side.
2. The arm should be in a half-bent position, parallel to the floor, palm up.
3. Body is then pivoted to the center line.
4. Suddenly straighten the body and whip the arm to the solar plexus.

THE BLOCKS FOR THE UPPERCUTS
1. Stepping out of range a few inches.
2. Dropping the open glove inward and downward across opponent's wrist or forearm, forcing the blow to the outside.

THE LONG UPPERCUTS
With a left step
1. Use the right hand to parry opponent's jab.
2. Step across the body with the left foot to a position outside of opponent's left foot.
3. At the same time drop the left hand perpendicular to the floor.
4. As the weight shifts forward, whip the left hand, palm up, to opponent's solar plexus.
5. The right hand is held off the left shoulder in position of guard.

With a right step
1. As above except step is taken with the right foot, one full step forward and to the side.

CHAPTER VI

THE ELEMENTS OF DEFENSE

DEFINITION

THE ELEMENTS OF DEFENSE are all techniques which are defensive in purpose and together give the whole concept of defense.

EXPLANATION

Boxing as a sport is characterized by a constant shift between attack and defense, each being important and depending upon the other for successful execution. Without attack there is no necessity for defense, and without defense there would be no attack. That a strong offense is supposedly the best defense is in general true, especially if defensive skill is the foundation of attack. Without underlying defensive strength there always comes a time when a good attack meets a better one. Then it is too late.

While hitting is the basis of all boxing, skill in defensive tactics makes it possible for the boxer to attack at the proper time. Defense then is the keynote of attack, and should be developed before attack.

USE

Blocking is the first line of defense. It means taking a blow on some part of the body which is less susceptible to injury. However, considerable resistance is necessary to block a hard blow which causes contusion of the tissue, nerves, and bone. Blocking, therefore, tends to weaken rather than conserve bodily forces. A well delivered blow, even if blocked, will disturb balance, prevent countering, and create openings for other blows.

Blocking may be used against all types of blows, either to face or body. It should be learned first and learned well. Later it should be used only when necessary.

Guarding is using the arms as levers to dispel the force of the opponent's blows and to obtain the inside position. Such movements require subtle judgment, speed, and coördination for their execution. Some contusion takes place, but not to the same degree as in blocking.

Guarding is used against straight blows and often as a lead-up to a counter-attack.

Parrying is a sudden movement of the hand from the inside or outside, onto an oncoming blow, to deflect the blow from its original path. It is a light, easy movement depending on timing rather than force. A blow is never parried until the last moment and always when close to the body. To reach out to parry a blow not only makes openings for counter blows, but enables the opponent to change the direction of his blow. Parry late rather than early.

Parrying is an extremely useful form of defense. It is easily learned, and easily performed, and should be used whenever possible. Advantageous openings are created which are essential to counter-fighting.

Stopping is the pinning of an opponent's hand or arm so that he is unable to deliver a blow. It may be used as a preventive measure when slipping or countering, or when an opponent actually intends to deliver a blow. Used in this manner, it requires a knowledge of when an opponent is going to lead, and depends on speed and skill for execution.

Slipping is avoiding a blow without actually moving the body out of range. It is used primarily against straight leads and counters. It calls for exact timing and judgment and to be effective must be executed so that the blow is escaped only by the smallest fraction. Performed suddenly the slip contains an element of surprise and leaves the opponent wide open at the mercy of a terrific counter-attack.

Because slipping leaves both hands free to counter, it is the method preferred by the expert.

It is possible to slip either a left or a right lead, although more often used and safer against a left lead. The outside slip, that is, to the right of an opponent's left lead, or to the left of an opponent's right lead, is the safest position, leaving the opponent unable to defend against a counter attack.

Slipping is an invaluable technique, the real basis of counter-fighting upon which depends the science of attack.

Ducking is dropping the body forward under hooks and swings to the head. It is used as a means of escaping blows allowing the boxer to remain in range for a counter-attack. Neither ducking, slipping, nor weaving should be practiced without hitting or countering.

It is just as necessary to learn to duck swings as it is to slip straight punches. Both are used for the same purpose, and both are important in counter-attack.

Weaving is an advanced defensive tactic which means moving the body in, out, and around a straight lead to the head, making the opponent miss and using the opening thus created as the start of a two-fisted counter-attack. Weaving is based on slipping and thus mastery of slipping helps to obtain skill in weaving. It is more difficult than slipping but a very effective defense maneuver once perfected. It is a circular movement of the upper trunk and head, right or left as desired.

Rolling means nullifying the force of a blow by moving the body with the blow. Against a straight blow, the movement is backward; against hooks, to either side; and against uppercuts, it is backward and away.

Rolling is often practiced by the expert, and it is almost impossible for a novice to hit an expert who is using it. It is a technique worth perfecting.

Sidestepping is shifting the weight and changing the feet without disturbing balance. It is used to avoid straight rushes forward, and to move quickly out of range of attack. It is a safe, sure, and valuable defensive tactic. It can be used to frustrate an attack simply by moving every time an opponent gets "set" to hit. It may be used as a method of avoiding blows or creating openings for a counter-attack.

Sidestepping may be performed by shifting the body forward which is called a forward drop. This is the safest position in boxing, that is, carrying the body and head to a place directly beneath the opponent's chest. Here, with the head in close, the hands carried high and ready to perform a double stop, is an area that is absolutely safe.

The same step may also be performed directly to the right or directly back, depending on the degree of safety needed or the plan of action. The sidestep should be perfected by every boxer.

Clinching means holding the opponent's arms in such a manner that he is unable to strike a blow. It is used as protection after missing a blow, when hurt or fatigued. However, it should be used only as a last resort. It slows up a match and makes clean, fast, skillful boxing impossible.

There are many means of clinching but only one which is absolutely safe and sure. All types should be practiced but this one should be perfected.

Covering is many times referred to as the safety block. It is the holding of the head in the crook of the right arm, while placing the left arm over the abdomen. It is not a recommended procedure and has no place in the tool kit of the skillful boxer.

The Rockaway means rocking the body away from a straight blow enough to make the opponent miss and as the opponent's arm relaxes to the body it is possible to move in with stiff counters. This is a very effective technique against a left jab and may also be used as the basis of the one-two combination blow.

THE TECHNIQUE OF DEFENSE

BLOCKING

This technique has been previously covered. However, because it is one of the elements of defense, it is herein included as a review.

Blocking with a glove is called a catch if used against a left jab. Instruction in its technique is given in Chapter III, page 17 (Figure 17). Against a right hook it is called a shoulder catch. Instruction in its technique is given in Chapter V, page 43.

Blocking with the elbow, against straight blows, is called the elbow block. Instruction in its technique is given in Chapter III, page 23 (Figure 30).

Against hooks and swings to the body, turn the body slightly with the blow, thus intercepting the blow on the elbow. The forearm must be straight and close to the body. The elbow is down and tight, hand protecting the face, chin down.

Blocking with the shoulder—Used against a straight right to the chin and called a shoulder block. For instruction in technique see Chapter III, page 20 (Figure 23).

Blocking with the forearm—is used against straight blows to the body. It is called the forearm block. For instructions in technique see Chapter III, page 25 (Figure 31).

GUARDING

The leverage guard—for instructions in technique see Chapter III, page 20 (Figure 22).

The leverage block is using the right arm as a lever against a straight left lead.

Assume the fundamental position. As the opponent leads a left jab, drive the right arm forward and sideways into complete extension, crossing on the inside of opponent's jab and forcing it wide of its mark.

The elbow must be completely straightened at the moment of contact with the opponent's forearm. Palm should be turned outward. Considerable force is necessary to keep the jab from coming through. The left arm is held in the position of guard or counter. Keep the chin down.

Parrying

The outside parry on a straight left lead—for instruction in technique see page 17 (Figure 18).

The outside parry on a straight right lead—Assume the fundamental position. As the opponent leads a straight right brush to the right with the left hand, striking opponent's oncoming blow on the wrist. The movement must be sudden and precise (Figure 55, page 53.) This parry is an arm movement as more force is needed to deflect the opponent's right arm inward. The left elbow, however, is not moved any more than necessary. Carry the right hand low, ready to counter.

The inside parry on a left lead—Assume the fundamental position. As the opponent leads a left jab, drop slightly to the left bringing the right hand to the inside of the oncoming jab. Turn the palm of the right hand outward, and brush the jab to the outside.

It is important to take a quick short step to the left with the left foot and bend the body slightly inside the left lead. The left hand should be ready to stop opponent's right counter. Keep the chin down. This parry calls for much practice and coördination in order to be properly executed (Figure 56, page 53).

The inside parry on a straight right lead—Assume the fundamental position. As the opponent leads a straight right, drop the body slightly to the right thus bringing the left hand well inside the lead. Turn the palm of the left hand outward and brush the right lead to the outside. The right hand is in position to block or counter (Figure 57, page 53). Considerable force is necessary for successful execution of this parry.

The cross parry on a straight left lead—Assume the fundamental position. As the opponent leads a straight left, reach over with the left hand and push the oncoming lead outward, causing it to go wide of its mark. The movement is primarily one of the wrist. The elbow does not move. Hold the right hand in position to counter to the body (Figure 58, page 53).

The cross parry on a straight right lead—For instructions in technique see page 22 (Figure 26).

FIG. 55. *Outside Parry on a Straight Right Lead*   FIG. 56. *Inside Parry on a Straight Left Lead*

FIG. 57. *Inside Parry on a Straight Right Lead*   FIG. 58. *The Cross Parry on a Straight Left Lead*

Parrying

STOPPING

Assume the fundamental position. Anticipate an opponent's lead and reach out with the glove and place it over the opponent's. In so doing, straighten the elbow and keep the body well out of range.

In slipping, ducking, and weaving always pin the opponent's right hand when moving to the inside position.

The stop for a right hook—For instruction in this technique see page 21 (Figure 25).

SLIPPING

The inside slip on the left jab—Assume the fundamental position. As the opponent leads a left jab, shift the weight over the left leg, thus moving the body slightly to the left and forward, and bring the right shoulder quickly forward. In so doing the left jab slips over the right shoulder, the right hip rotates inward and the right knee bends slightly. The movement gains the inside position which is the best position for attack. The left hand is placed over the opponent's right. The head is moved only if the slip is too close (Figure 59, page 54).

FIG. 59. *Inside Slip on a Left Jab*   FIG. 60. *Outside Slip on a Straight Left Lead*

Slipping

The inside slip on a straight right—This technique is the same as used in slipping to the outside position on a straight left lead. Assume the fundamental position. As the opponent leads a straight right, drop the weight back to the right leg by quickly turning the left shoulder and body to the right. The right foot remains stationary but the left toe pivots inward. This movement allows the right lead to slip over the left shoulder and obtains the inside vantage position.

Carry the left hand high, ready to counter to the face or body. The right hand should be held ready to block opponent's left counter, and to prevent this, place the open right glove in the crook of opponent's arm.

The outside slip on a straight left lead—Assume the fundamental position. As the opponent leads a left jab, drop the weight back to a straight right leg by quickly turning the left shoulder and body to the right. The right foot remains stationary but the left toe pivots inward. The left jab will slip harmlessly over the left shoulder.

Drop the left hand slightly but hold it ready to hook to opponent's body. The right hand should be held high off the left shoulder ready to counter to the chin (Figure 60, page 54).

The outside slip on a straight right lead—is almost the same as the inside slip on a straight left lead. Assume the fundamental position. As the opponent leads a straight right, step forward and sideways with the left foot, shifting the body weight over the left leg. At the same time, turn the right shoulder smartly forward. The right hip swings forward and the right leg bends slightly. The left hand is carried to the right of the chin, and the right hand is dropped to waist position ready to counter with a right uppercut to the body.

DUCKING

The same technique is used to duck either right or left swings. Assume the fundamental position. As the opponent leads a hook or swing bend the trunk forward from the waist, and at the same time dip both knees forward so that the body is practically dropped. This will carry

FIG. 61

Ducking

the body underneath the hooks which will swing harmlessly over the head.

Both hands should be carried high, elbows down. From this position counters can easily be executed. The chin is pinned tight to the breast bone leaving only the top of the head vulnerable (Figure 61, page 55).

WEAVING

To the inside position—Assume the fundamental position. On a left lead slip to the outside position (Figure 64, page 56). Drop the head and upper body and move in under the extended left lead and then up to the fundamental position. The left lead now approximates the right shoulder (Figure 62, page 56). Carry the hands high and close to the

FIG. 62. *To Inside Position* (1)   FIG. 63. *In Between Position* (2)

FIG. 64. *To Outside Position*
Weaving

body. As the body moves to the inside position, place the open left glove on opponent's right. Later, counter with a left blow, then a right and left as the weave is performed.

To the outside position—Assume the fundamental position. As the opponent leads a left jab slip to the inside position (Figure 62, page (56). Move the head and body to the right and upward in a circular movement so that the opponent's left lead approximates the left shoulder. The body is now on the outside of the opponent's lead and in and fundamental position (Figure 64, page 56). Both hands are carried high and close. As the inside slip is executed, place the left glove on the opponent's right. Later, counter with both hands as slip is performed.

WEAVING PRACTICE

Have number 1's place their extended left arm so that it rests on number 2's left shoulder (Figure 64, page 56). 2's then duck the head to the left and under 1's extended left arm so that the arm rolls across to the right shoulder (Figures 63, 62, page 56). Repeat, rolling first inside, then outside.

ROLLING

With straight blows—As the opponent leads, lean the body backward with the blow so as to dissipate its force.

With bent-arm blows—As the opponent leads, turn the body so it will travel in the same direction as the blow. On right swings, bend or swing body to the right. On left swings, bend or swing the body to the left. On uppercuts, merely sway backward out of range.

SIDESTEPPING

Assume the fundamental position (Figure 65, page 58). Slide the left foot back until the toe is pointing toward the right heel (Figure 66, page 58). Move one full step to the right with the right foot shifting the body-weight over the straight right leg (Figure 67, page 58). The right foot controls the direction of the step, either directly sideward, obliquely sideways and backward, or directly backward.

To start with, the weight is either forward or distributed between the legs. It is then transferred to the right leg. The foot positions are now reversed, the right foot being flat and pointed directly to the side with the heel of the left foot off the floor and the toe pointed the same way as the right foot. Between these stages, when the left foot is dropped back to the right heel, the weight is barely taken up by the left foot. Therefore this intermediate stage is like stepping on a tack, very little weight is placed on the foot. Once the weight is shifted to the straight right leg, all that is necessary to return to attack is to pivot on the balls of the feet to the left, and shift the weight back to the left leg (Figure 65, page 58).

FIG. 65   FIG. 66   FIG. 67

The Side Step

CLINCHING

It is important in clinching to grasp the hands or arms but not the body. The only sure way to find the arms or hands is to start holding at the shoulders and move the hands down the arms. To do this both hands must start from the inside position.

As the opponent leads a left, move both hands forward in a manner similar to a breast-stroke movement in swimming. From the opponent's shoulder move the left hand down and around his right biceps and at the same time move the right hand down to his left elbow, forcing his left glove-hand up and under the right armpit. Continue to hold the opponent's left elbow with the right hand (Figures 68 and 69, page 59). As the arm is locked under the armpit, turn the body to the right and drop the weight on opponent's right arm. If the opponent tries to get loose, spin him off balance by merely walking forward, using his left arm as a lever.

Another method is to place the open hands around both of the opponent's biceps. As the opponent tries to hit, throw weight against the biceps, tipping him off balance and rendering his effort impotent.

If there is no other way out, throw both arms around the opponent and hold tight. Keep the body close and the arms locked tight.

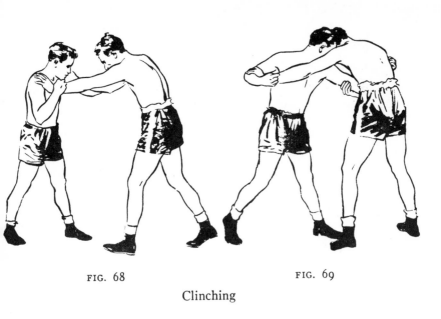

FIG. 68   FIG. 69

Clinching

A double lock may be used by pushing both of the opponent's gloves up and under the armpits and then locking the hands in front of the body.

In clinching it is important to keep the body as close to the opponent as possible. Do not allow the opponent to move away. Stay close until the referee orders a break. If possible, keep the left shoulder against opponent's chest, and the left leg close to his body. In this manner there is little chance of punishment. Only when coming into or going out of a clinch is a boxer liable to "get hurt."

In breaking a clinch keep the hands high and well extended until the opponent is out of range. By placing the left hand behind the opponent's left elbow, and the right hand in back of his left shoulder,

give a quick push with the left hand and a pull with the right, spinning
the opponent off balance.

THE ROCKAWAY

As the opponent leads a left jab or a straight right, shift the weight
quickly to the right leg, and move back with the opponent's blow. As
the blow falls short and his left hand folds back to the body, step in
with a left jab, and follow by a straight right.

FUNDAMENTALS OF FORM

BLOCKING

The catch

1. Catch opponent's left lead in the butt of the open right glove.
2. Force the blow up and out, thus obtaining the inside position.
3. Hold the left hand ready to attack.

The shoulder catch

1. Catch the opponent's right hook in the open right glove.
2. Hook the thumb of the right hand in the crook of the left
   shoulder.
3. Lower the left hand slightly, ready to counter.

The elbow block

1. Turn the body so that either elbow will intercept straight leads
   to the body.
2. Elbows should not move but should be held tight to the body.
3. Arms are carried close and protect the head; chin down.
4. Hands should be held ready to counter.

Shoulder block

1. Use against a straight right hand.
2. Turn the left shoulder so that it intercepts the left lead.
3. Drop the weight back to a straight right leg so that the left shoulder is tilted upward.
4. Lower the left hand, ready to counter over the opponent's right
   lead.

The forearm block

1. Use against straight blows to the body.
2. Fold the left arm under, right arm above.

3. Hold the forearms together, palm-side of the hand turned toward the body.
4. The chin is exposed so be ready to fold underneath if necessary.

GUARDING

The leverage block
1. Use against a straight right lead.
2. Force must be used if guard is to be effective.
3. Force the left arm up and outward into complete extension.
4. At the moment of contact with opponent's arm, lock the elbows.
5. Hold the right hand ready to stop opponent's left or to counter.

The leverage guard
1. Use against a straight left lead.
2. Straighten the right arm upward and outward, striking opponent's lead from the inside and forcing it outward.
3. Lock the elbow at the moment of contact.
4. Turn the right hand outward.
5. Force must be applied to the guard.
6. Hold the left hand in a position of guard, ready to block opponent's right or to counter to face or body.

PARRYING

The outside parry on a left jab
1. Brush the opponent's lead to the left with the right hand.
2. The movement is more wrist than arm.
3. Do not move the elbow.
4. Intercept the opponent's oncoming blow on the wrist, not the glove.
5. Lower the left hand, ready to counter to opponent's body.

The outside parry on a straight right lead
1. Brush the opponent's right lead to the right with the left hand. Step to the left and forward at the same time.
2. Use force with arm as well as wrist.
3. Do not move the elbow more than necessary.

The inside parry on a straight left lead
1. Drop the body slightly to the left bringing the right hand inside the left lead.

2. Brush outward with the right hand, palm turned outward.
3. Hold the left hand ready to block or counter.

The inside parry on a straight right lead
1. Turn the body slightly to the right.
2. Brush outward with the left hand.
3. Turn the palm of the left hand outward.
4. Carry the right hand ready to block or counter.

The cross parry on a straight left lead
1. Reach over with the left hand and brush the opponent's left lead outward.
2. Perform the movement with the wrist and arm.
3. Move the elbow only as much as necessary.
4. Lower the right hand ready to counter.

The cross parry on a straight right lead
1. Reach over with the right hand and brush opponent's right lead outward.
2. Perform the movement with the wrist and arm.
3. Move the elbow only as much as necessary.
4. Be ready to fold forward under opponent's left counter lead.

STOPPING
1. Reach out and place the hand over opponent's glove.
2. When slipping, ducking, or weaving, pin the opponent's right hand.

SLIPPING
The inside slip on a left jab
1. Shift the weight over a straight left leg.
2. Turn the right shoulder forward.
3. Swing the right hip forward, with the right knee bent and loose.
4. Place the left glove over opponent's right glove.

The inside slip on a straight right
1. Shift the weight over a straight right leg.
2. Turn the left shoulder through to the center line.
3. Hold the right foot stationary with the left toe turned inward.

4. Hold the left hand ready to counter.
5. Drop the right hand over the opponent's left glove.

The outside slip on a straight left lead

1. Shift the weight over a straight right leg.
2. Turn the left shoulder and hip to the right.
3. Keep the right foot stationary, left toe pointed inward.
4. Lower the left hand ready to counter to the body.
5. Hold the right hand off the left shoulder in a position to guard or counter.

The outside slip on a straight right lead

1. Take a short step forward and sideways with the left foot.
2. Shift the weight over the left leg.
3. Let the right shoulder, hip, and leg swing forward to the left.
4. Lower the right hand ready to counter to the body.
5. Carry the left hand right of the chin.

DUCKING

1. Use against swings and hooks.
2. Bend the trunk forward from the waist and dip both knees forward thus dropping the body downward under the hooks.
3. Carry the hands high, chin well down.

WEAVING

To the inside position on a left lead

1. Slip to the outside position.
2. Drop the head forward and bend the trunk slightly.
3. Move the head to the left, under opponent's arm and up to position.
4. Carry both hands high and in position of guard.
5. As the body moves to the inside position, place the left glove on opponent's right.

To the outside position on a left lead

1. Slip to the inside position.
2. Drop the head forward and bend the trunk slightly.
3. Then move the head to the right, under opponent's arm and up to position.
4. Carry the hands high.

ROLLING

1. Move the body backward with the straight blows.
2. Move the body to the left on left swings or hooks.
3. Move the body to the right on right swings or hooks.

SIDESTEPPING

1. Move the left toe back to the right heel, the left toe pointing directly towards the right heel.
2. Take one full step to the right with the right foot, shifting the weight to the right leg.
3. The foot positions are now reversed and the body turned directly to the side.
4. From that position step out or
5. Pivot back to attack by turning on the balls of the feet to the left and shifting the weight back to the original stance position.
6. Carry the hands high, in position of guard.

CLINCHING

1. From the inside position, run the hands down to opponent's gloves.
2. Place the open left glove around opponent's right biceps.
3. Tuck the opponent's left glove up and under the right armpit and close arm to the side.
4. Shift the weight to opponent's left arm.
5. No matter what form of a clinch is used, keep close to the opponent until the referee calls for a break.

THE ROCKAWAY

1. Use against a left jab.
2. Drop the weight to the right foot, moving the body back with the jab.
3. As the jab falls short and returns to the body, move in with a left and right to the chin.

THE ELEMENTS OF ATTACK

DEFINITION

THE ELEMENTS of attack are all techniques which are used to carry attack by strategy. They are the devices and skills of the finished boxer. Requiring speed, deception, timing, and judgment, they are the tools of the master craftsman who blends them into perfect attack.

EXPLANATION

Attack is based upon the fundamental ability to hit and to defend, and upon such advanced skills as slipping, ducking, weaving, parrying, and guarding. Once a boxer has mastered the different blocks and blows, it is necessary for him to be able to create openings which will enable him to score. This is the reason for the study of offense.

In general, there are two methods of attack, either by force or by deception and strategy. Attack by force or aggression is the attack of the unskilled, the novice. This type of attack may be successful because any continuous attack tends to keep the opponent so occupied that openings result. Such a boxer is the "mauler" or "slugger" who depends mainly on hitting power, demonstrating no crisp hitting, clever footwork, or "finishing" ability.

Attack by deception is the attack of the master. The master boxer has at his command techniques to bewilder and confuse the opponent, thereby creating many openings. He feints his opponent into "knots." He combines hitting with feinting in such a manner that both appear to be the same. He draws his opponent to him forcing whatever leads he desires. Through defensive hitting and judicious movement, he keeps his opponent off balance. The master boxer has the ability to get in close and understands the value of infighting. He has so perfected the "shift" that it is used for attack as well as defense. Finally, he is the master of counter fighting for he knows when to attack and when to allow attack.

Scientific attack then is no simple matter, but requires years of study and practice for its successful use.

USE

Leading—The master of attack must know the value of a straight lead. He must know what is liable to happen on any lead. He realizes that for every lead there is an opening, and for every opening, a counter, and for every counter a block. These things he understands but he also knows how and when to lead with comparative safety.

Leading with the left hand, guarding with the right while moving to the left, makes negligible any opening that ordinarily results from a straight left lead.

Feinting—is characteristic of the expert boxer. It requires using the eyes, the hands, the body, and the legs in a single effort to deceive an opponent. These movements are really decoys and if the opponent attempts to adjust his defense, the expert takes advantage of the openings created. Feinting is also used to ascertain what the opponent's reactions will be to each movement.

Feinting creates only momentary openings. To be able to take advantage of the openings created means instant reflex action, or foreknowledge of what openings will be created by certain feints. Such familiarity presupposes practice, for only through the actual practicing of many feints against many kinds of opponents may a general reaction tendency be determined.

In boxing, as in football, an opening should be "set up." Once an opening is created by a certain feint, that opening should not be used until a clean sure blow will result.

A good boxer knows what openings will result before he feints, and makes use of this knowledge and initiates his follow-up action almost before the opening results. Whenever two boxers of equal speed, strength, and skill are matched, the one who is the master of the feint will be the winner.

The essential elements in feinting are rapidity, change, deception and precision, followed by clean crisp blows. Feints used too often in the same way will enable the opponent to time them for a counter attack, thus defeating their very purpose.

Feinting is the art of using the body in feinting attack at one point, and then attacking another. It involves footwork, knees, hands, eyes, arms, and trunk. Feints against the unskilled are not as necessary as against the skilled. Many combinations of feints should be practiced until they are natural movements.

Drawing—is closely allied to feinting. Whereas in feinting an opening is created, in drawing some part of the body is left unprotected in order that a particular blow will be led by the opponent thus developing an opportunity to use a specific counter. Feinting is only a part of drawing. Drawing uses the method of strategy, and the method of crowding or forcing. Being able to advance while apparently open to attack, but ready to counter if successful, is a phase of boxing that few ever develop. Many boxers refuse to lead. Then to be able to draw or force a lead becomes very important.

Infighting—is the art of boxing at close range. Not only does it take skill to get in close, but it takes skill to stay there. To get inside, it is necessary to slip, weave, duck, draw, or feint. When obtaining the inside position, drive both hands to the opponent's midsection.

The Drop Shift—is a further refinement of the sidestep. It is used to gain the inside or outside guard position and is also useful in infighting. Mainly a vehicle for countering, it requires timing, speed, and judgment to properly execute. It may be combined with the left jab, the straight right, the right hook, and the left hook.

THE TECHNIQUE OF ATTACK

THE SAFETY LEAD

Assume the fundamental position. Shuffle forward to attack. As the hitting range is approached, jab with the left hand while stepping to the left, and at the same time force the right arm out into the position of a leverage guard. Carry the left shoulder high to protect the chin from the opponent's right hand. Hold the right hand in readiness for the opponent's return jab.

FEINTING

It is best to practice feinting before a full-length mirror. Practice each method and notice the deception of each.

Assume the fundamental position. Advance slowly. While advancing, give a quick bend of the left knee. This gives the impression that the arms are moving as well as the legs. In reality, the arms are held relaxed and ready.

Make a slight forward movement of the upper body, bending the left knee and moving the left hand slightly forward. While advancing, take a longer step forward with the left foot, as in the quick advance, and jab the left arm into extension without hitting the opponent. From this close position, fold the left arm back to the body and jab to the chin.

Another effective feint is a short bend of the body to the right while moving forward.

The step in, step out, feint means stepping forward one step as if to jab with the left hand but, instead, step out of range by pushing off with the left leg, pivoting to the left. Now step in as if to feint but drive a left jab to the chin. Step out immediately. Continue, one time feinting, the next time actually jabbing with the left hand. If possible, follow the left jab with a straight right to the chin.

Other feints that may be used are: Feint a left jab to the face and jab to the stomach; feint a left jab to the stomach and jab for the face; feint a left jab to the face, feint a right to the face and then jab the left to the chin; feint a straight right to the jaw and hook the left to the body; feint a jab to the chin and deliver a right uppercut to the body.

DRAWING

By exposing the body to attack—To draw a left-hand lead to the jaw, carry the right hand low, exposing the chin to the opponent's leads. As the opponent leads, step either in or out, countering with either hand.

To draw a left lead to the body, raise the right elbow. Be ready to drop a right-hand blow to opponent's chin, or to step inside of the lead with a straight right.

To draw a right-hand lead to the head, lower the left hand and be ready to slip inside or out, leaving either hand free to counter.

To draw a right-hand lead to the body, raise the left elbow, or carry the left elbow high. Be ready to brush or cross-parry the opponent's right lead.

By forcing—Assume the fundamental position. Slowly shuffle to the attack which usually brings a left lead. Be ready to slip inside or outside countering either to body or face.

Shuffling forward and exposing a particular part of the body is a method used to force a specific lead. Therefore, if a left-hand lead to the body is desired, shuffle forward holding the right elbow high.

By feinting—Experience alone will tell which feint to use in order to draw a specific blow. Only practice will give knowledge of what blow each feint will draw.

INFIGHTING

Assume the fundamental position. Draw a left lead and slip to the inside position, hands carried high. Place the head on the opponent's breastbone and push forward. This will force the opponent on to his heels and off balance. At the same time, drive short uppercuts to his midsection. Keep the arms in the inside position, and keep driving them (Figure 70, page 69). Stay close, for if the inside position is kept,

FIG. 70

Infighting

it is possible to shift with the opponent. As the opponent leads a right for the body, drive the left inside his blow and to the body. As the opponent shifts to deliver a left, drive the right inside and to the body. Continue, pommeling the body until the opponent drops his guard, then suddenly shift the attack to his head.

If the opponent obtains the inside position and starts to pommel the body, place the open palms of both hands against his shoulders. Push slightly forward, sliding the right hand to the side of the opponent's left shoulder and force to the left while pushing forward with the left hand. This will spin the opponent off balance.

THE DROP SHIFT

This is executed similar to the sidestep. As the opponent leads a straight left, slide the left foot back six inches, and at the same time step forward one full step with the right foot (Figures 71 and 72, page 70). The weight shifts to the right leg. The foot positions are reversed, the right foot is flat on the floor, and the toe of the left foot is off the floor. As the body shifts forward to avoid the lead, a counter attack may be started.

FIG. 71   FIG. 72

The Drop Shift

The shift, forward or sideward, may be combined with the left jab, the left hook, or the straight right. On the forward shift, as the weight is shifted to the right leg, jab with the left hand. A longer reach and more power will result. On the side shift, as the weight is shifted to the right leg, hook the left hand to the opponent's chin. Tremendous power may be obtained in this way. On the side shift, after the weight has been shifted to the right leg, turn the body quickly back to position, and drive a straight right to the opponent's jaw.

FUNDAMENTALS OF FORM

THE SAFETY LEAD

1. Step left on a left jab.
2. Hold the right arm well extended, palm turned outward.
3. Be ready for opponent's right counter.

FEINTING

1. Always "build up" an opening before making use of it.
2. Feints must be precise of action, rapid, and decisive.
3. Each feint will bring a characteristic reaction. Know this reaction before feinting. This necessitates practice.
4. Do not always use the same feint. Change is important.
5. Feint with the whole body.

DRAWING

1. This is an advanced art and depends on speed, timing and judgment.
2. A blow may be drawn by exposing the body, by forcing, or by feinting.
3. Drawing depends on the counter attack for effectiveness.
4. It is a necessary knowledge against an opponent who will not lead.

INFIGHTING

1. The inside position must be obtained through slipping, weaving, ducking, and drawing.
2. Place the forehead on the opponent's breastbone.
3. Force forward with the head pushing the opponent off balance.
4. Keep driving both hands to the opponent's solar plexus.
5. Maintain the inside position at all times.
6. Shift with the opponent.
7. If the opponent drops his arms, switch the attack to the head. Use short arm-jolts.

THE DROP SHIFT

1. Move the left foot back six inches and take one full step forward, shifting the weight to the right leg.
2. May be effectively combined with a left jab.

CHAPTER VIII

THE COUNTER ATTACK

DEFINITION

COUNTER ATTACK means fore-knowledge of specific openings which will result from attack by the opponent. The counter attack is not a defensive action but a method of using an opponent's offense as a means to the successful completion of one's own attack.

EXPLANATION

The counter attack is an advanced phase of offense. It calls for the greatest skill, the most perfect planning, and the most delicate execution of all boxing techniques. It uses as tools all the main techniques of boxing, blocking, guarding, parrying, slipping, weaving, ducking, sidestepping, feinting, drawing, and shifting. It uses all phases of hitting, crisp, straight blows, clean hooks, and short uppercuts. Besides a mastery of technique, the counter attack requires exact timing, unerring judgment, cool, calculating poise. It means careful thought, daring execution, and sure control. It is the greatest art in boxing, the art of the champion.

There are numerous counters which may be used for every lead, but for each particular occasion there is one counter which should be used. Such a counter is that one most effective for the particular situation at hand. Action must be instantaneous, and where there is a wide choice of action, instant action is difficult if not impossible unless the right action has been previously conditioned. Conditioning then becomes the keystone of the counter attack.

Conditioning is a process whereby a specific stimulus will cause a specific reaction. A repeated stimulus eventually creates an action pattern in the nervous system. Once this pattern is established the mere presence of the stimulus will cause a specific action. Such action is instantaneous and almost unconscious which is necessary for effective countering. In boxing, conditioned action should be the result of intense and concentrated practice of planned action patterns in response to every lead. Such action should be practiced slowly, for hours, days, and weeks, always in response to certain leads. Finally, the lead itself will automatically bring the right counter.

Boxing should be done with the head, not with the hands. It is true that during the time of actual boxing one does not think of how to box but rather of the weakness or strength of the opponent, of possible openings and opportunities. Boxing will never reach the stage of a true art unless performance of skill is made automatic and the cortex freed to think and to associate, to make plans and to judge. The higher nerve centers always retain control and will act when necessary. It is like pressing a button to start or stop a machine.

In a consideration of counter blows there are three things that must be understood:

    a. the lead of the opponent.
    b. the method of avoiding the lead.
    c. the counter blow itself.

The lead of the opponent is important in that it determines the side of the body open to attack. A left lead exposes the left side of the body, while a right lead exposes almost all of the upper trunk.

To avoid leads it must be decided whether the counter attack should be one- or two-handed. Blocking, guarding, stopping, parrying, all leave but one hand with which to counter. Such maneuvers as slipping, sidestepping, ducking, weaving, feinting, drawing, and shifting allow a two-handed attack.

The counter blow depends upon the method used in avoiding the opponent's lead as well as the lead itself. In other words, if the opponent jabs and the blow is avoided by an inside slip, a right to the heart or a right cross is indicated.

USE

The Inside Parry and Left Jab—is a straight left so timed as to take advantage of the opening left by the opponent's jab. It is a fundamental counter used consciously or unconsciously by almost every boxer. It is used to avoid the opponent's jab and at the same time sting and jar him. It is also used to "set up" openings for other counters. It is best used against a slow left jab.

The Outside Parry and Jab—is a jab delivered after slipping the opponent's lead over the left shoulder. It is a safe way to avoid a left lead while dealing out punishment at the same time. It is best used against the long-armed opponent as it adds length to the left arm. The left jab is parried and held momentarily to the left shoulder. The more the opponent steps in with his jab, the more severely he will be punished. It should be used in combination with jabbing from the inside position.

The Inside Block and Right Hook—is first a block and then a blow. It should be used against a slow jab or the boxer who carries his left hand well out from the shoulder. It is a powerful blow but requires more practice and more accurate timing than most counters. It requires blocking a left lead from the inside, then shifting the weight forward and hooking the right to the chin. It is not advisable to use unless the opening is very apparent.

The Straight Inside Right—is a straight right timed to cross under and inside an opponent's left lead. It is best used against an opponent who steps well in with his left lead. It then becomes a "set-up" or finishing blow. It is an easy blow to time, carries terrific power and is best used in conjunction with the outside parry and left jab or a right cross. The left hand must be carried high in position to stop or guard.

The Right Cross—is one of the most talked of blows in boxing and the counter most often used by all boxers. Delivered properly, it exerts terrific force. It is merely a right hook to the jaw crossed over an opponent's straight left lead. The opponent's jab is slipped over the right shoulder and the right hand then hooked from the outside across to the chin. It is easy to execute and is really a finishing blow.

The Inside Right to the Heart—is a "sucker" punch in that it takes advantage of a natural opening created by any left lead. It is difficult to guard against. It is a straight right timed so as to drive underneath an opponent's left arm as he jabs, and is used to slow up an opponent or to "shorten his arms."

The Outside Parry and Left Hook to the Body—This is used to bring down the opponent's guard, to create openings for the right hand, and to slow up an opponent. It is easy, safe, and effective. It is really an uppercut rather than a hook.

The Inside Parry and Left Hook to the Liver—is a jarring, sickening blow used to slow up an opponent. It is rather dangerous to execute as it brings the body into range of the opponent's right hand. As the left hand and shoulder is dropped, the left side of the body becomes a target for the opponent. Therefore, it must be used suddenly and depends entirely upon speed and deception for its success.

THE TECHNIQUE OF THE COUNTER ATTACK

It should be realized at this time that it is impossible to perfect all counters. Every counter requires hours of study and practice, and takes years to perfect. To try to perfect too many counters means perfecting none. Select those counters that seem easiest to perform and surest in result, and concentrate upon them.

There are eight elementary counters that every boxer should know. Out of the eight, at least four should be made automatic in execution. While only eight counters will be given, there are over seven hundred possibilities. A few of the most common counters are listed below.

LEFT HAND COUNTERS FOR A STRAIGHT LEFT LEAD

By Blocking or Stopping

1. On a straight left lead, catch the opponent's lead in the right glove, at the same time stepping left and drive a straight left to the chin.

By Parrying

1. On a straight left lead, parry to the outside guard position and hook the left to the solar plexus.
2. On a straight left lead, parry to the outside guard position and hook the left to the chin.
3. On a straight left lead, parry to the outside guard position and deliver a left uppercut to the chin.
4. On a straight left lead, parry to the inside position and drive a straight left to the chin.
5. On a straight left lead, parry to the inside guard position and hook the left to the solar plexus.
6. On a straight left lead, parry to the inside guard position and uppercut left to the solar plexus.

By Slipping

1. Slip to the outside position and hook the left to the chin.
2. Slip to the outside position and hook the left to the solar plexus.
3. Slip to the outside position and drive a left uppercut to the solar plexus.
4. Slip to the outside position and drive a straight left to the chin.

By Sidestepping
1. Sidestep to the outside position and drive a left hook to the chin.
2. Sidestep to the outside position and drive a left hook to the solar plexus.
3. Sidestep to the outside position and drive a left uppercut to the chin.
4. Sidestep to the outside position and drive a straight left-hand to the chin.

RIGHT-HAND COUNTERS FOR A STRAIGHT LEFT LEAD

By Parrying
1. On a straight left lead, parry to the inside guard position with the right hand, then drive the right hand to the opponent's chin.
2. Cross parry the opponent's left lead with the left hand and drive a straight right to the opponent's side.

By Slipping
1. On a straight left lead, slip to the inside guard position and hook the right to the heart.
2. On a straight left lead, slip to the inside guard position and drive a straight right to the heart.
3. On a straight left lead, slip to the inside guard position and drive a straight right to the chin.
4. On a straight left lead, slip to the inside guard position and cross a right hook to the opponent's chin.
5. On a straight left lead slip to the inside guard position and drive a right to the solar plexus.

By Sidestepping
1. Sidestep to the outside guard position and drive a right cross to opponent's chin.
2. On a straight left lead, sidestep to the outside guard position and drive a right to the heart.
3. On a straight left lead, sidestep to the inside guard position and drive a right uppercut to the chin.
4. On a straight left lead, sidestep to the outside guard position and drive a right uppercut to the chin.
5. On a straight left lead, sidestep to the inside guard position and drive a right uppercut to the solar plexus.

Left-Hand Counters for a Straight Right Lead

By Parrying

1. On a straight right lead, cross parry with the right hand and hook left to the chin.
2. On a straight right lead, reach across with the right hand and parry the lead to the outside, hooking the left hand to the opponent's abdomen.

By Slipping

1. On a straight right lead, slip to the inside guard position and hook the left to the solar plexus.
2. On a straight right lead, slip to the inside guard position and cross a left hook to the chin.
3. On a straight right lead, slip to the outside guard position and cross-left to chin or body.

By Sidestepping

1. On a straight right lead, sidestep to the inside guard position and drive a straight left to the chin.

Right-Hand Counters on a Straight Right Lead

By Parrying

1. On a straight right lead, parry to the inside guard position with the left hand, then drive a straight right to the chin or body.
2. On a straight right lead, parry to the inside guard position with the left, then hook the right to the chin or body.
3. On a straight right lead, parry to the inside guard position with the left and drive a right uppercut to the chin or solar plexus.
4. On a straight right lead, parry to the outside guard position with the left and hook the right to the chin or solar plexus.
5. On a straight right lead, parry to the outside guard position with the left and drive a right uppercut to the chin or solar plexus.

By Slipping

1. On a straight right lead, slip to the outside guard position and drive a right hook to the chin or body.
2. On a straight right lead, slip to the outside guard position and drive a right uppercut to the chin or body.
3. On a straight right lead, slip to the outside guard position and drive a straight right to face or body.

4. On a straight right lead, slip to the inside guard position and drive a left uppercut to the solar plexus.

By Sidestepping

1. On a straight right lead, sidestep to the outside guard position and hook the right to the chin or body.
2. On a straight right lead, sidestep to the outside guard position and drive a right uppercut to the solar plexus.

THE INSIDE PARRY AND LEFT JAB

Assume the fundamental position. As the opponent leads a straight left, step forward and left with the left foot, turning the left shoulder directly forward and driving the left arm into complete extension. The right arm is carried high, hand turned out, parrying the left lead outward. Start slowly and speed up as skill is attained (Figure 73, page 78).

THE OUTSIDE PARRY AND LEFT JAB

Assume the fundamental position. As the opponent leads a left jab, parry and momentarily pin to the left shoulder. At the same time jab the left hand out into extension, using the forward shift to give power. The right hand is held high and ready to counter after first parrying (Figure 74, page 78).

FIG. 73. *Inside Parry and Left Jab*   FIG. 74. *Outside Parry and Left Jab*
Fundamental Counters

THE INSIDE BLOCK AND RIGHT HOOK

Assume the fundamental position. As the opponent jabs with left, lean slightly to the left and at the same time raise the right forearm inside opponent's left and block lead to the outside (Figure 75, page 79). Then tip the right elbow up in a straight line with the opponent's chin, step forward and sideways with the left foot, shifting the weight to the left leg, and drop a right hook to the opponent's chin (Figure 76, page 79). Carry the left hand in the position of guard. Start very slowly and speed up as the movement is coördinated.

FIG. 75. *Inside Block and Right Hook* (1)   FIG. 76. *Inside Block and Right Hook* (2)

Fundamental Counters

THE INSIDE RIGHT TO THE JAW

Assume the fundamental position. As the opponent leads a left jab, quickly turn the body to the left, bringing the right shoulder forward to the center line (Figure 77, page 80). From this point drive the right hand into complete extension. The left lead slips to the outside of the right arm. The left hand is held in the position of guard (Figure 78, page 80). A short step to the left, shifting the weight over a straight left leg may be used to obtain more power.

THE RIGHT CROSS

Assume the fundamental position. As the opponent leads a straight left, slip to the inside position by stepping forward and sideways with the left foot, shifting the weight over a straight left leg. Keep the right hand outside the opponent's guard. As the opponent's jab slips over the right shoulder, the right arm, now in a half-bent position, is hooked over the opponent's left lead to the chin. The left hand is carried high and in a position of guard (Fig. 79, page 80). The whole action is performed as if it were one. Be sure to hook over and down.

FIG. 77. *Straight Inside Right to Chin* (1)

FIG. 78. *Straight Inside Right to Chin* (2)

FIG. 79. *The Right Cross*

FIG. 80. *The Inside Right to the Heart*

Fundamental Counters

The Inside Right to the Heart

Assume the fundamental position. On the opponent's left lead, slip to the inside position and drive a straight right to the heart. The body is low and on the same plane as the right arm, the arm protecting the head. The left hand is held high and ready to stop the opponent's right hook (Figure 80, page 80). To obtain the greatest power, step forward and left six to eight inches with the left foot, while shifting all the weight over the left leg.

The Outside Parry and Left Hook to the Solar Plexus

Assume the fundamental position. On the opponent's left lead, parry to the outside position with the right hand. At the same time drop the left arm perpendicular to the floor (Figure 81, page 81, and step across with the right foot to a position outside opponent's left foot. As the weight shifts over the right leg, hook the left hand to the solar plexus.

This same movement may be repeated by stepping across with the left foot to a position outside the opponent's left foot (Figure 82, page 81).

FIG. 81. *Outside Parry and Left Hook to the Solar Plexus —Right Step*

FIG. 82. *Outside Parry and Left Hook to the Solar Plexus —Left Step*

Fundamental Counters

THE INSIDE PARRY AND LEFT HOOK TO THE LIVER

Assume the fundamental position. As the opponent leads a straight left, drop directly to the left and to the inside guard position. Parry the left lead outward with the right hand (Figure 83, page 82), pivot sharply from the waist, forcing the left hand up and under the opponent's guard to the solar plexus (Figure 84, page 82). The weight is shifted over the left leg which becomes a pivot around which the body wheels on completion of the blow.

FIG. 83. *Inside Parry and Left Hook to Liver* (1)

FIG. 84. *Inside Parry and Left Hook to Liver* (2)

Fundamental Counters

FUNDAMENTALS OF FORM

THE INSIDE PARRY AND LEFT JAB

1. Shift the weight over a straight left leg.
2. Turn the left shoulder straight forward.
3. Drive the left hand into complete extension.
4. At the same time parry the opponent's left lead outward with the right hand.

THE OUTSIDE PARRY AND LEFT JAB

1. Use the right hand to parry opponent's left lead inward.
2. Momentarily pin the left lead on the left shoulder.
3. At the same time shift forward and jab the left to the chin. The jab is outside the opponent's lead.
4. Hold the right ready to counter.

The Inside Parry and Right Hook
1. Lean slightly to the left.
2. Parry the left lead outward with the right hand.
3. Step forward and to the left with the left leg, shifting the weight forward.
4. At the same time raise the right elbow and hook to opponent's chin.

The Inside Right to the Chin
1. Shift the weight to a straight left leg.
2. Turn the right shoulder and hip to the center line.
3. Drive the right arm under the opponent's left lead to the chin.
4. Carry the left hand high and ready to stop the opponent's right counter.

The Right Cross
1. Step forward and left with the left leg without moving the right arm.
2. Shift the weight to the left leg allowing the opponent's lead to slip over the right shoulder.
3. Hook the right arm up and over the opponent's extended arm to the chin.
4. The left hand should be placed over the opponent's right hand in order to prevent a counter blow.

The Inside Right to the Heart
1. Take one step forward and sideways with the left foot.
2. Shift the weight to the left foot, turning the hip and shoulder through to the center line, allowing opponent's left to slip over the right shoulder.
3. Drive the right hand inside of the opponent's left lead, to the heart.
4. Carry the left hand high and ready for the opponent's left counter.
5. Protect the head with the right arm.

The Outside Parry and Left Hook to the Solar Plexus
1. Parry the opponent's left lead to the outside with the right hand.
2. Drop the left arm perpendicular to the floor and step across to

a position outside the opponent's left foot with the left or the right foot.

3. Shift the weight to the front leg and then hook the left hand to the solar plexus.
4. Carry the right hand high, ready to cross to the chin.

THE INSIDE PARRY AND LEFT HOOK TO THE LIVER

1. Step forward and left with the left foot.
2. Parry a left lead to the outside with the right hand.
3. At the same time shift the weight to the left leg and drive a left uppercut to opponent's liver.
4. Using the left leg as a pivot, wheel the body left and out of range.

CHAPTER IX

SET-UPS

DEFINITION

THE TERM "SET-UPS" denotes a series of blows delivered in a natural sequence. The object is to maneuver the opponent into such a position, or create such an opening, that the final blow of the series will find a vulnerable spot thus rendering the opponent helpless and "setting him up" for the finishing or knockout blow.

EXPLANATION

The difference between an expert and a novice boxer is that the expert makes use of each opportunity and follows up each opening. He delivers his blows in a well-planned series, each opening creating another, until finally a clean "shot" is obtained.

Some blows seem to be "follow" blows in that they come after certain leads. For instance, the straight right is a "follow" blow for the left jab, and a left hook is a "follow" blow for the straight right.

It seems natural to punch straight and then hook and it seems natural to punch first to the head and then to the body. "Follow" blows or "set-ups" have rhythm and "feel" as their basis. Punching in rhythm is an important factor in boxing.

Every boxer should make use of a natural sequence. To be sure that a sequence will be used while boxing, it is necessary to practice punching in sequence. Any combination of blows may be used as long as openings are created. Each individual may set up for himself a series of blows which will work effectively. There are, however, a few series of blows which are of proven value, and should become a part of every boxer's tool-kit.

USE

The Triple Blows—are combinations of three different punches which have slipping as their basic technique. Always the first two blows are to the body, followed by a blow to the chin. There are two triples, one which starts with a slip to the inside guard position, and one which starts with a slip to the outside guard position. Both are effective, but the inside triple is used more often. Jack Dempsey used this triple to "hit 'em in the stomach, then hit 'em on the jaw." The first two blows are designed to bring down the guard to create an opening for the final or finishing blow.

The One-two-three Sequence—is a series of three blows which have as their basis rhythm, timing and power. They are blows which seem to follow each other naturally. One series, that is, the jab, cross, and hook, is intended to narrow the opponent's guard and create an opening for a hook from the outside. The jab, hook, and cross series is designed to create an opening for a final straight blow to the chin. Both series can be used effectively.

The High-Lows—are a series of blows which have rhythm as their basis in punching first to the body and then to the head, or vice versa. The wide hook is used to open a path for the final straight blow. The main thing to remember is that the last blow will be to the spot of the first blow. If the first blow is to the jaw, the last blow will also be to the jaw.

THE TECHNIQUE OF THE "SET-UPS"

THE INSIDE TRIPLE

Assume the fundamental position. As the opponent leads a left jab, slip to the inside position with a right to the heart (Figure 85, page 87). Then weave under the opponent's extended left arm and as the weight of the body shifts to the right leg, hook the left hand to the solar plexus (Figure 86, page 87). From this outside position, cross the right to the opponent's chin (Figure 87, page 87).

More power may be obtained if a short step to the right is taken with the right foot after the inside right is delivered. This carries the head and body under the opponent's lead and to the outside guard position, shifting the weight over the right leg as the left hand is hooked to the opponent's midsection. The body is then straightened, weight shifted to the left leg and the right hand crossed to the opponent's chin. The left hand is carried high and close, in position of guard.

THE OUTSIDE TRIPLE

Assume the fundamental position. As the opponent leads a left jab, drop underneath to the outside position and swing a wide left hook to

FIG. 85. *The Inside Triple* (1)

FIG. 86. *The Inside Triple* (2)

FIG. 87. *The Inside Triple* (3)
The "Set-Ups"

the opponent's midsection. The right hand should be open and carried off the left shoulder (Figure 88, page 88). Step in and to the left with the left foot, carrying the body under the opponent's left lead and hook the right hand to the heart. The left hand is dropped over the opponent's right glove (Figure 89, page 88). From this position straighten the body and lift the left hand to the opponent's chin. The right arm is carried off the left shoulder, open and in position of guard (Figure 90, page 88).

FIG. 88. *The Outside Triple* (1)

FIG. 89. *The Outside Triple* (2)   FIG. 90. *The Outside Triple* (3)

The "Set-Ups"

THE ONE-TWO COMBINATION

Because the one-two is the basis of the straight-blow combinations, it is essential to understand its technique.

Assume the fundamental position. Step forward with the left foot and jab with the left hand (Figure 16, page 16). Move the right foot to position and drive the right hand into complete extension (Figure 21, page 19). The rhythm is important and should be *o-n-e two!*

THE JAB-HOOK

This is also a basic combination blow. Assume the fundamental position. Jab with the left hand. Hold the left arm in the extended position until the weight shifts back to the straight right leg. Then hook the left arm in an arc for the right shoulder.

THE JAB-STEP AND HOOK

Assume the fundamental position. Jab the left arm into extension. Without moving the left arm farther, walk toward the left hand. This forces the arm to bend at the elbow. The arm is now in a half-bent position. Drop the weight back to the right leg and hook the left arm in an arc to the right shoulder. The right hand should be carried high and in position of guard.

THE JAB-CROSS AND HOOK

Assume the fundamental position. Drive a one-two to the chin (Figures 16, 21, pages 16, 19). Then take one short step to the right and hook the left to the chin. The right hand should be carried high in position of guard (Figure 91, page 90).

THE JAB-HOOK AND CROSS

Assume the fundamental position. Jab with the left hand, then shift the weight to the right leg and hook the left to the chin. Rock the weight forward to the left leg and drive a straight right to the chin. The left arm is held close to the body in position of guard (Figures 16, 91, 21, pages 16, 90, 19).

THE STRAIGHT HIGH-LOW

Assume the fundamental position. Fling the left hand forward and upward in front of the opponent's face. Drop suddenly by bending the right knee and twisting the body to the left. As the right shoulder and hip turn through to the center line, drive the right arm out into extension, to the opponent's heart. The left arm folds to the body in a position of guard.

THE HIGH-LOW AND CROSS

Assume the fundamental position. After jabbing several times, step in with a left hook to the face (Figure 91, page 90). Allow the opponent time to anticipate the next move, a left hook to the body (Figure 92, page 90. As the opponent drops his hands to protect his midsection, drop a short straight right to the chin (Figure 93, page 90). The rhythm is *one ... one-two.*

FIG. 91. *The High and Low Cross* (1)   FIG. 92. *The High and Low Cross* (2)

FIG. 93. *The High and Low Cross* (3)

The "Set-Ups"

The Low-High and Uppercut

Assume the fundamental position. Step in with a wide hook to the body (Figure 94, page 91). Hesitate so that the opponent will anticipate a hook to the chin. Then hook to the chin (Figure 95, page 91) and follow immediately with a right uppercut to the solar plexus (Figure 96, page 91). The rhythm is the same, *one . . . one-two.*

FIG. 94. *The Low-High and Uppercut* (1)

FIG. 95. *The Low-High and Uppercut* (2)

FIG. 96. *The Low-High and Uppercut* (3)

The "Set-Ups"

FUNDAMENTALS OF FORM

THE INSIDE TRIPLE

1. Use only against a left lead. Action must be fast and continuou
2. Slip inside with a straight right to the heart. Use a stop for tl opponent's right.
3. Step sideways with the right foot, moving the foot up even wi the left.
4. At the same time, shift the weight over the right leg and hoo the left hand to solar plexus.
5. Straighten the body and cross the right to the opponent's chi weight shifting to the left foot.
6. Keep the body low until the final movement. Weight is shifte first to the left leg, then to the right leg, and back again to tl left leg.

THE OUTSIDE TRIPLE

1. Use on a left lead.
2. Bend the body to the right under the left lead and hook the le to opponent's midsection.
3. Move the left foot sideways and forward as the body move to the inside guard position.
4. Hook the right to opponent's ribs, at the same time stopping th opponent's right with the left hand.
5. Then straighten the body and whip the left hand to opponent' chin.
6. Keep the body low until the final blow. The weight is shifte from the right foot, to the left, and then back to the right.

THE ONE-TWO

1. Jab with the left hand and step with the left foot.
2. Follow by moving the right foot to the fundamental position and driving the right arm out into complete extension.
3. The rhythm is *o-n-e-two*.
4. Be sure to jab high with the left hand, thus blocking vision Then drive the right hand to the chin.

THE JAB-HOOK

1. Jab with the left hand.
2. Without moving the hand, shift the weight back to the right foo and hook the left hand in an arc toward the right shoulder.
3. Hold the right hand off the left shoulder.

The Jab-Step and Hook

1. Jab, without stepping with the left foot.
2. Hold the arm extended and walk to the arm. Elbow is thus bent to position of a hook and held off the left shoulder.
3. Whip a short hook to opponent's chin.
4. Perform the movement fast. Successful execution depends upon deception and speed.

The Jab-Cross and Hook

1. Drive a one-two to the opponent's chin.
2. Then step to the side with the right foot, and whip a left hook to the opponent's chin.

The Jab-Hook and Cross

1. Use the jab-hook to the chin, weight shifting back to the right leg with the hook.
2. Shift the weight to a straight left leg and drive a straight right to the opponent's chin.
3. Fold the left arm close to the body in a position of guard.

The Straight High-Low

1. Fling the left arm upward and forward.
2. Quickly drop the body forward and drive a straight right to the heart.
3. Hold the left arm ready to stop the opponent's right-hand blow.

The High-Low and Cross

1. Remember that if the first blow is high, the last blow is high.
2. Lead a wide hook to the chin. Hesitate, and hook to the body. Then drop a straight right to the chin.
3. The rhythm is *one . . . two, three.*
4. The first two blows are designed to clear the path for the last blow.

The Low-High and Uppercut

1. Lead a wide left hook to the body. Hesitate, then hook a left to the chin. Follow immediately with a right uppercut to the solar plexus.
2. Rhythm is the same, *one . . . two, three.*

RING CRAFT AND RING GENERALSHIP

DEFINITION

RING CRAFT is the ability to meet and successfully solve problems as they arise in the ring. Ring generalship is a general plan of battle thought out in advance of the bout, which attempts to nullify the opponent's strength and take advantage of his weakness.

EXPLANATION AND USE

Ring craft means the faculty to successfully adapt oneself to the opponent's style. It means the ability to out-smart and out-think the opponent in the ring. Ring craft depends upon knowledge, skill, physical condition, and experience to guarantee good performance. While a boxer may be naturally wary and cautious and show a tendency toward good ring craft from the very beginning, a real ring master is one who is wise in the ways of the ring, who knows the situations that are most likely to occur and how best to meet them.

In general, ring craft means ascertaining as soon as possible the opponent's weakness or strength, his favorite mode of attack and his general manner of defense. It means learning the opponent's moves, his timing and his whole style of boxing. It means making the opponent fight in any way desired, to tire him out and frustrate his attack.

Ring generalship means a general knowledge of boxing styles and the most successful way of meeting each style. A plan of battle may be mapped out before a bout. If this is done, it necessitates knowing exactly what style of boxing the opponent uses. It is probably best to map out the exact plan of battle after boxing a round or more so that the plan will fit the style the opponent is using at the moment.

THE TECHNIQUE OF RING CRAFT

There is no special technique of ring craft. Experience seems to be the only teacher although in general, there are certain techniques which have proven useful to many. These techniques are hereby presented as ring stratagems.

RING STRATAGEMS

1. Use your head—fight with your head, not your hands. Out-think the other man and you can out-hit him.
2. Be in condition—nothing will make up for good physical condition.
3. Relax! Tenseness tightens and slows reaction time. Don't try too hard.
4. Know the fundamentals—there will be many chances to use them.
5. Appear confident at all times. If hurt or tired, don't show it.
6. Never forget that the opponent is as tired or as afraid as you are.
7. The left hand is the safest lead. Use it.
8. Keep moving or stand still and be hit. However, do not jump around or make unnecessary movements.
9. Carry the hands high at all times.
10. Keep the chin tucked to the breast-bone.
11. Punch the moment the opponent is in range. Otherwise, you will be punched. Don't save punches!
12. If a blow is missed or you are unbalanced, clinch and wait for the referee to break.
13. Puzzle the opponent by a variety of maneuvers. Never do the same thing twice in succession.
14. Once the inside guard position is gained, stay close and punch.
15. Never underestimate an opponent. Remember, they are all tough.
16. Keep the feet under the body at all times. When off balance the body is open to attack.
17. Hit hard when you hit! Mean business. Snap a blow, don't push.
18. Punch only when there is an opening. Don't punch just to be doing something.
19. Punch *through* an object, not *at* one.
20. Step in to hit. It is impossible to hit hard while moving backward.
21. Do exactly what the opponent doesn't want done.
22. Never stop trying. Remember, it only takes one.
23. The safest place in boxing is in close, head waist-high, hands high.

24. There are two times when you are most likely to get "hurt," either coming into attack, or going out.
25. Whenever the opponent gets set to hit, move.
26. Note carefully what the opponent does preceding his leads.
27. Make a mental note of any peculiarities.
28. The natural counter for a left jab is a right cross, therefore act accordingly.
29. Realize that ordinarily a straight punch will "beat" a hook.
30. The two-handed attack to be effective must start from the inside position.
31. The outside guard position is the safest place.
32. Right-hand leads and short hooks are counter blows. Unless you want to get hit, do not lead them.

THE TECHNIQUE OF RING GENERALSHIP

Because generalship is primarily concerned with a plan of action against different styles of boxing, some of the styles will be herein considered.

How to Box a Tall Opponent

This situation is often encountered. A tall man has more to protect, often he is slower and therefore there are more openings. However, to offset these disadvantages, the tall man has reach and probably considerable power.

In general, the best plan is to keep moving in and out, in an attempt to draw a left lead. On the lead, slip in fast, countering hard and often. Once in, place the forehead on the opponent's chest and force him backward and off balance. At the same time lift short arm jolts to the solar plexus.

One method of deception is to gradually edge the left foot nearer the opponent without altering the position of the head. With the stance spread it will be easier to reach the opponent.

How to Box a Croucher

Any opponent who continually crouches is a difficult man to hit effectively. He fights from a "shell," well covered up.

Some crouchers bend directly forward. In this case, use speed, stepping in and out with short inside uppercuts. Never stay in close.

If the opponent crouches to either the left or the right side, jab to the front shoulder and try to force or spin him off balance. If this is done, follow up and stay close, taking advantage of each opening.

How to Box a Rusher

The rusher is chronic to the sport of boxing. He is the unskilled who must force himself close in order to score.

The sidestep was made for the rusher. As the opponent rushes, sidestep and deliver a counter blow.

Another effective method is to step in with a straight one-two to the chin. As the opponent rushes, step smartly forward with the left foot and drive the left hand to the chin. Follow with a straight right. Once in close, clinch, resting the weight on the opponent. Wait until the referee breaks. As opponent rushes again, repeat.

Straight blows will score before swings and hooks. Keep the blows high, chin down. If a hit is scored, follow up, if missed, clinch.

How to Box a Jabber

Some boxers use only one blow, the left jab. To cope with this style, keep the body low. The inside position must be obtained by slipping, weaving, or sidestepping. Punch while going in, a right to the heart or a left hook to the body. Once in close, pin the forehead on the opponent's chest and stay there. Drive both hands to the opponent's body.

The ability to fold under a left jab is an effective way of moving in close. As the opponent leads, drop the head into the crook of the right arm. This forces the jab over the top of the head. Carry the left hand low, ready to counter.

How to Box a "Southpaw" (left-handed boxer)

Special technique is required to box a "southpaw." There are three principles that should be followed: (1) make the southpaw lead first; * (2) circle to the left, away from the southpaw's left hand, and (3) use the right hand as the major weapon of offense. As a general rule this will bring good results. It should be varied as circumstances indicate.

Circling left against a "southpaw" nullifies his best hand, his left. A "southpaw" usually has a terrific power in his left hand, which he

---

* Many coaches and seconds maintain that the proper method is to carry the attack to a "southpaw." From knowledge gained in handling "southpaws" it has been found that they prefer the attack to be carried to them. It seems that if they are forced to lead, they leave themselves open, and are off balance.

invariably hooks. By circling away from the left hook, not only is power nullified, but a better position is obtained from which to deliver a right counter. However, a right hook may be encountered. If possible, "feint out" the right hook. Usually on a feint, the "southpaw" will draw back his right arm ready to cross. When he does, step in with a straight left arm, hand open, to the opponent's right biceps or shoulder. This will spin him off balance and into a right counter.

THE SLUGGER

Some men are endowed with the ability to hit and hurt with either hand. These men seldom take the trouble to learn how to box or to hit straight. They depend mainly on powerful hooks. They are always dangerous opponents.

Heavy hitters must "get set" in order to deliver their blows, therefore to keep moving is the best defense. Inability to "get set" will lessen the hitter's power and make it less dangerous. Moving around does not mean jumping but simply means moving efficiently and easily to prevent the opponent from getting ready to hit. Each time the opponent stops to hit, move. Such a plan will render his attack ineffective.

A good piece of strategy is to suddenly stop moving and step quickly in on the opponent, catching him unprepared and off balance. This must be done swiftly, moving in and out before the opponent can "set" himself to hit. Do not attempt to "slug" with him.

A boxer who stands still is a "catcher." Move constantly, in and out, not vigorously, but easily.

THE COUNTER FIGHTER

The counter fighter is a dangerous opponent. He turns the force of his opponent's blows back against the opponent. A counter fighter depends upon leads of the opponent. Therefore do not lead, and especially do not lead the blows expected. If possible, force the counter fighter to lead by feinting or drawing. If this does not work, do what he expects, only be ready to counter the counter blow.

An aggressive attack with speed and power is an effective method in some cases. Such a procedure keeps a counter fighter off balance and thus ineffective.

A crouch is very effective against a counter fighter. Get down low, bob and weave, but do not lead. If opponent does not lead rush in fast driving both hands in fast. Once in, stay in.

FUNDAMENTALS OF FORM

How to Box the Tall Man
1. Keep moving.
2. Draw a left lead.
3. Slip to the inside guard position.
4. Commence infighting.

How to Box a Croucher
1. Sidestep and counter.
2. Step in with a one-two to the chin.
3. If a hit is scored, follow up. If the blows are missed, clinch.

How to Box a Jabber
1. Keep low.
2. Slip to the inside or outside guard position.
3. Counter to the body.
4. Try to time a right cross.
5. Force continually.

How to Box a "Southpaw"
1. Don't lead, make the "southpaw" come to you.
2. Circle left, away from the opponent's left hook.
3. Use the right hand to the face or body, straight or hooked.

How to Box a Slugger
1. Keep moving, don't let the opponent get set.
2. Attack suddenly.
3. Move out immediately, don't slug.

The Counter Fighter
1. Make him lead if possible.
2. If he won't, do what he expects and counter his counter.
3. Keep him off balance by a whirlwind attack.

CHAPTER XI

HOW TO TRAIN FOR BOXING

TRAINING is one of the most neglected phases of athletics. Too much time is given to the development of skill and too little to the development of the individual for participation. The body is treated as if it were an object and subject to definite rules and regulations. Nothing could be further from the truth. Training deals not with an object, but with the human spirit and human emotions. It, takes intellect and judgment to handle such delicate qualities as these.

Training is the psychological and physiological conditioning of an individual preparing for intense neural and muscular reaction. It implies discipline of the mind and power and endurance of the body. It means skill. It is all these things working together in harmony.

Training means not only knowledge of the things which will build the body, but also knowledge of the things which will tear down or injure the body. Improper training will result in injuries. Training then is concerned with the prevention of injuries as well as first-aid to injuries.

I. CONDITIONING

PSYCHOLOGICAL CONDITION

An individual may have all the physical gifts possible—speed, co-ordination, and power. The body may be ready for extreme exertion, yet the individual may be a poor competitor. It is easy to prepare the body for a contest; it is difficult to prepare the mind. It is necessary to help each individual discipline his thinking, to help him control his emotions, to dispel fear and worry.

Fear—is one of the most important considerations in athletic conditioning. It is especially important in boxing. There are many boys who are timid, shy, afraid. They are afraid to box. They are afraid of any activity in which there is any personal contact. In reality, they are only afraid of the idea of being hurt, not of actually being hurt. The task is to get them to prove this fact to themselves.

This type of boy must not enter the ring before receiving certain protective experiences. He should have a strong defense and some successful boxing experience.

Careful handling from the beginning will develop sureness and confidence in the boys. They will find out that it does not hurt to be hit. When this stage is reached, fear is forgotten. The problem then is to keep these boys from being entirely reckless in this new-found confidence. Boys who start out in tears from fear of boxing, will, inside of a few months, be the most eager and usually become the best students in the class.

Mind discipline—Conditioning of any sort means discipline, discipline of the will and through the will, the body.

Training rules and habits are most useful for their disciplinary value. Discipline in conditioning means creating an attitude, a mind set toward a desired end. The end results are really the most important, training only the means to the end. Discipline is the method.

If the end object is really important enough, any rules or regulations will be followed. It becomes increasingly important, then, to stress procedures which lead not only to proficient skill in boxing, but to right attitudes and habits of health and life.

Training should be made a strict discipline. It will require things which seem difficult, monotonous, and dreary. It will necessitate giving up many things—ease, comfort, and all forms of dissipation. It takes a strong incentive to be able to enforce such an existence but in so doing a boy is given a training in concentrated effort toward a goal and an inkling of the price that is required in the attainment of any goal. Build up the end result so that it looms above all else in the mind of the boy. If this is done completely, there can be built into that individual any type of health habit or attitude desired.

Physiological Condition

Diet—To understand diet is to understand nutrition. Briefly, nutrition means the process of digestion, absorption, assimilation, heat and energy release, the discarding of waste materials, and finally, the rebuilding of the cell and the storing of an excess of cell food.

Digestion is the chemical and mechanical breakdown of food. It starts in the mouth through the action of the teeth and salivary juices. It is continued in the stomach by the action of the various gastric juices, the pyloric mill and further aided in the intestine by the pancreatic juices and peristaltic action.

By this time the food is in a state of liquid chyme. In this form it is passed from the intestine into the plasma of the blood through the process of osmosis. As the plasma bathes all the cells of the body the food is assimilated directly by the cell. The cell stores the food as fuel until there is a demand made upon it. In muscle contraction, food is used, heat, water and energy liberated, and waste matter thrown off. Then the demand for food is repeated.

Protein, minerals, and water are tissue builders and rebuilders. Carbohydrates produce energy and liberate heat. Fat is stored in the body as fat and used only if there is a lack of carbohydrates in the diet. Excessive carbohydrates store in the body as fat. Of all the food elements, protein, alone, cannot be stored.

Thus a diet for an athlete should be heavy in proteins and sugar, and low in fats. The carbohydrates should exceed the protein in the diet by almost three to one.

The diet should be so planned that an alkalinity of the tissues results. A diet that produces an excess of acid is incorrect because alkalinity tends to increase wind and endurance. An athlete preparing for competition should eat lean meats, milk, fruit and leafy vegetables. Such rich foods as cream, fried foods, fat meats, rich cake or pastry should be avoided. The sugar content of the diet may be increased during training or just before a contest.

In boxing, orange juice just before a bout, or between contests may be used. Glucose candy is beneficial if it can be obtained.

Water—is a most important factor in conditioning. Dehydration will result due to profuse perspiration induced by physical exertion. Water should be used freely both inside and out to replenish that lost during a workout. However, in all cases, water should be taken sparingly twenty-four hours before a contest.

It is necessary to abstain from all use of coffee, tea, and alcoholic beverages during training. Smoking should not be allowed.

The *pre-contest diet* is important. No food should be taken later than four hours before a contest. Food in the stomach at the time of the contest tends to cause nausea and indigestion.[1]

Food that is eaten should be light but nourishing. A small portion of sirloin steak, or two soft-boiled or poached eggs, or two broiled

[1] Dr. John Stephan Lewis, as quoted by Trevor C. Wignall, et al., *The Story of Boxing*, p. 220.

lamb chops, or a small portion of broiled chicken, with two slices of dry toast and a cup of weak tea is all that should be eaten.

Sleep and relaxation—Sleep and relaxation is as necessary to an athlete as correct diet or special training. Boxing, or any strenuous activity, breaks down the cells, liberates lactic acid and other waste products into the blood, and uses stored-up energy. Sleep is the period when nature replenishes. An athlete needs a great deal of sleep because he is exercising strenuously and because he is usually young and growing.[1]

Sleeplessness may occur before or after a contest. A good book, a quiet movie, congenial company, with light discussion and laughter all help to relieve tension. A hot foot-bath, or a warm tub-bath of about body temperature for fifteen or twenty minutes are effective methods of relieving insomnia.

After a strenuous contest, a good soaking tub-bath not only dispels tension, but will tend to dissipate soreness from the muscles. Fill a tub with water, not more than ninety degrees Fahrenheit. Empty into the tub three to five pounds of epsom salts.[2] Stay fifteen minutes or longer.

It is important to realize the value of frequent rests during the actual training period. Not only is the interest held, and learning heightened, but efficiency is maintained longer.[3]

Elimination—Proper elimination is essential in the conditioning of athletes. A certain "habit time" is of utmost importance to regularity and should be stressed. The plain, simple life of the athlete, wholesome food, plenty of exercise, are controls in themselves. All that is needed is to create a habit. Cathartics are weakening and if taken at all, should not be taken within two days of contest.

Exercises for conditioning—The greatest exercise for conditioning in boxing is roadwork. If an athlete has time for only a single training activity, that activity should be roadwork. Running strengthens the heart, the lungs, and the legs. The heart will be able to adjust to the strenuous exertion, the lungs will be better able to supply more oxygen and the legs will be better able to support the body during a bout. How far to run and how to run, is the question. The long jog is no

---

[1] Dr. Walter Meanwell, and Knute K. Rockne, *Training, Conditioning and Care of Injuries*. Madison, Wisconsin, 1931, p. 82.

[2] Salt tends to raise the temperature of the water a few degrees. Therefore, do not start with the water too warm.

[3] Coleman Griffith, *The Psychology of Coaching*, p. 82.

longer considered of any value. Too much energy is used, it tears down rather than builds.

The new method is that of "wind sprints." Sprint one hundred yards and then walk one hundred yards. Continue until the desired distance is covered. Start with a quarter mile and gradually increase until a mile can be covered. When sprinting, run with all possible speed.

Many boxers find it best to run the same length of time as they will box, resting one minute between runs. For instance, if preparing for three, two-minute rounds, run at top speed for two minutes, then walk a minute. Repeat three times.

The aspiring boxer must be made to realize that each part of his body must be exercised and strengthened as much as possible. The extensors of the arms, the abdominal muscles, and the neck muscles should receive special attention.

The arms are used continually. They tire easily unless specially trained. The abdominal region is the "mark" for which all boxers try and therefore well-developed muscles are essential. The neck must be able to absorb the shock of head blows. A strong neck is a protection that should not be overlooked. The following exercises are especially adapted for the boxer:

Neck Exercises

1. *The wrestler's bridge*—Take a supine position on the mat. Fold the arms across the chest. Bring the legs well up underneath the body. Now using just the head and legs as supports, raise the body clear of the floor. Roll back on the forehead. Repeat.

2. *The front bridge*—Take a prone position on the mat. Place the top of the head on the mat. Using the head and legs as supports, bend the body forward and up. Repeat.

Stomach Exercises

1. *The sit up*—Assume a supine position, hands outstretched over the head. Raise the trunk to a sitting position, then force it down between the legs. Repeat. Start with ten repetitions and work up to twenty-five.

To increase resistance, fold the arms across the chest. Start at ten repetitions and work up to twenty-five.

For further resistance, use a light weight back of the neck. Start with ten repetitions and work up to twenty-five.

2. *The leg raise*—Assume a supine position. Raise the legs slowly until they are directly above the eyes. Lower slowly. Repeat ten to twenty-five times.

3. *Knees to chest*—Assume a supine position, arms outstretched over the head. Raise the knees to the chest while bringing hands over to clasp the knees. Ten to twenty-five times.

4. *The jack-knife*—Take the supine position, arms outstretched over the head. Sit up and bring the arms over in an attempt to touch the toes as they are raised off the floor.

5. *The alternate leg raise*—Take the supine position. Place the hands under the hips, palms down. Raise the head and pin it to the breast-bone. Raise the legs alternately back and forth as fast as possible. After forty repetitions have been reached, assume a sitting position and repeat.

6. *The double leg circle*—Take the supine position. Holding both legs together circle them first to the right, then to the left. Make a complete circle, low and wide. Start five times one way, then five times the other way. Practice until the exercise can be performed twenty times each way.

ARM EXERCISES

1. The triceps muscle of the arm is the main extensor muscle of the arm. One of the best exercises to develop that muscle is the "push up" from the floor. Assume the prone position, hands flat on the floor, shoulder-width apart. Keeping the body in a straight line, straighten the arms out, raising the body from the floor. Do not let the body sag. Repeat as many times as possible.

Staleness—is the result of overwork and neural fatigue.[1] Lack of pep, listlessness, no interest or enthusiasm, and irritability all are evident signs. Loss of weight is the best objective sign. There is only one remedy; complete rest and change. If you feel stale stay away from practice until you really feel like working.

II. SPECIALIZED TRAINING

Specialized training consists of those activities which deal with the actual process of learning boxing skills, or obtaining boxing condition.

[1] Meanwell, *op. cit.*, p. 61.

Pulley weights—are valuable as a physiological "warm-up" period. It is a time, too, when attention is narrowed, and concentrated. The weights should be used to loosen and stretch all the muscles of the body. Work on the weights should be methodical. Exercise facing the pulleys and with the back toward the pulleys. Shadow-box in both positions. Work fast and smooth so that the weights do not jerk. Work vigorously. Keep the chin down. Work according to rounds, with a minute rest between.

Rope skipping—is especially good for the feet, ankles, and legs. It is a fair developer of "wind" due to the fact that big muscles of the body are called into action. Too much rope skipping tends to tense the shoulder muscles. Jump one round, then rest a minute. Continue.

The light bag—has little use in a boxer's routine. It is impossible to hit a light bag correctly and therefore tends to develop bad hitting habits. It is little aid in the development of timing as it is almost entirely a matter of rhythm. Work on the light bag will strengthen the hitting muscles of the shoulders and arms and has some value in developing a left jab and in shortening a straight right lead. However, the blows should be practiced individually, not in rhythm.

The heavy bag—is valuable in the early training of a boxer. The primary purpose of the heavy bag is the development of hitting-power, and the strengthening of the hands, wrists, and arms.

A definite routine of blows should be used. Practice each blow for form, then for power. Perfect one blow at a time before proceeding to another.

The hands should be well protected when using the heavy bag. Toward the final stages of training, the heavy bag should not be used. There is too much danger of injury to the hands, and it tends to reduce speed reaction.

Shadow-boxing—is the best method of acquiring correct form. Shadow-boxing should be used to perfect boxing skill. It teaches ring movement, hitting sequence, speed, and relaxation. Each blow should be practiced and perfected before going on to another. It is best to shadow-box in front of a mirror so that the movements can be watched for correct form. Once form is obtained, greater speed and power should be the aim.

Shadow-boxing should be used to habituate each new technique given in a lesson. Shadow-box according to rounds. Don't loaf. Move deliberately in, out, and around. Punch hard all of the time. Plan each round before attempting to shadow-box. Then follow the plan. Other than actual boxing, it is the most important technique in the acquisition of boxing skill.

Boxing—The best practice to learn how to box is boxing. During an actual round of boxing work toward some definite objective. Don't ever box just to be boxing. Never play or "fool around." Stop as soon as fatigue sets in.

Box with all types of individuals, tall, short, slow, and fast. Timing and judgment of distance can only be developed through actual boxing.

Box according to a set number of rounds, always resting one minute between rounds. Try to learn something from each man boxed. Two or three times a week is enough actual boxing. Spend the rest of the time perfecting skills.

Roadwork—A few of the principles of roadwork are:
1. Run the same number of rounds as will be boxed.
2. If a three-round bout is being prepared for and the rounds are to be two minutes in length, run two minutes at top speed, then walk a minute. Continue three times.
3. As wind and endurance improve, try to increase the distance covered in the same length of time.
4. When starting to train, run every day. If in condition, three times a week is enough, preferably on off-training days.
5. Dress warmly. Run with the hands high. During the minute of rest, keep swinging the arms.
6. Run in the morning if possible. Remember, wind-sprints are best.

Drying out—is abstinence from liquids for a period of twenty-four hours before a bout. It is not a method of "making weight." It is used to increase speed and endurance. A pound or so of weight will be lost in the process, but that is incidental and not the reason. Physiologically, drying out is increased ionization of the body which means increased electric conduction of nervous energy. The body is like a storage battery. It must have water to operate. In the body, as in the battery, there is a certain possible ionization. Up to a degree, the less water, the greater the ionization. The result is an increase in endurance, power, and speed.

It is advisable for all athletes to abstain from liquids twenty-four hours before a contest. Thirst may be relieved by washing the mouth out, or by sucking a lemon. No actual liquid should be taken from the time the drying out process starts until *after* the contest.

Making weight by the process of dehydration is not a desirable procedure in any sport. Every person has a natural weight for best performance. This weight can be reached through regular conditioning methods. A weight other than that which is natural is detrimental to a boy's health and should not be allowed. It defeats the whole educational purpose of the activity. It is the game that is important, not the winning, and the individual rather than the activity, therefore be sure that every boy understands the purpose of dehydration.

The work-out procedure—The boxing work-out is an individual matter, and should be governed by condition and needs. Endurance should be stressed in training for long bouts. In contests of short duration, speed is of the most importance.

Each work-out should be entered into with a purpose. It should be planned beforehand with a specific idea in mind. During the work-out, work at full speed and when tired, stop. Always stop when feeling fresh and desiring more. If fatigued before the scheduled time, stop anyway. Skip a day if feeling low and tired. Fatigue causes careless work, and therefore the formation of bad habits. It is during these times that accidents occur. Always work out according to accurately-timed rounds. Relax during the minute rest.

A General Work-out Program
  Round 1—Warm up on the pulley weights.
  Round 2—Skip rope.
  Round 3—Work on the heavy bag.
  Round 4—Box.
  Round 5—Shadow box.
  Round 6—Calisthenics.

The total time for the work-out is only eighteen minutes. Work at top speed all the time. Take a hot shower while still perspiring.

Six weeks should be allowed to get into condition for a match. The first two weeks should be devoted to general conditioning, mainly roadwork and calisthenics. The last four weeks should be spent in specialized work-outs. At no time should more than one hour actual working time be spent in a gymnasium.

3rd week—Spend considerable time on the heavy bag working for power. Some boxing should be done.

4th week—Form should be stressed through shadow-boxing. Boxing should be increased.

5th week—Boxing should be stressed although a lot of shadow boxing should be used. Taper off from heavy bag-work.

6th week—Shadow-boxing for speed is now important. Boxing should be discontinued. The heavy bag should not be used. Rest at least one day before the contest.

III. THE PREVENTION OF INJURIES

There have been many objections raised against boxing but perhaps the foremost is that boxing is a dangerous sport.

People in actual contact with the sport know that it is not dangerous. Perhaps an occasional sprained thumb, a black eye, a broken nose, a split lip, or a chipped or broken tooth, but no permanent scars or injuries. The injuries that do occur are minor and are not serious.

Frank Lloyd, George Deaver, and Floyd Eastwood in their study on safety [1] found boxing to be an activity of minimum hazard in high school with an incidence of less than one accident per thousand opportunities. In college, the incidence of accidents increased to 4.6 per thousand opportunities. In a listing of sports according to incidence of accidents boxing was seventh, with football, horse polo, wrestling, lacrosse, soccer and crew more hazardous.

Teeth injuries were the most serious with sprains of the arms and hands next in order of frequency. That injuries in boxing are of a minor nature is borne out in the listing of activities according to days lost from school per thousand exposures. Boxing is listed tenth with 3.9 days lost, with only lacrosse, baseball, and tumbling having a better record.

The study indicates that accidents in athletics are low generally in comparison with other fields,[2] and that merely staying at home is more hazardous than participation in athletics.[3] With boxing listed as hazardous in a listing that includes highly hazardous and very hazardous, *and*

---

[1] Frank S. Lloyd, George Deaver, and Floyd Eastwood, *Safety in Athletics, The Prevention and Treatment of Athletic Injuries.* New York: Saunders and Company, 1937, p. 87.

[2] *Ibid.,* p. 24.

[3] *Loc. cit.*

if athletics in general is less hazardous than staying at home, then surely boxing is a safe sport for any boy.

Injuries in boxing are due mainly to inadequate leadership, which includes poor officiating, supervision, and conditioning, and to improper equipment.[1]

EQUIPMENT AND FACILITIES

Space—Space for boxing should be large enough so that a ring may be erected, and such apparatus as heavy and light bags, pulleys, exercise mats and free exercise space should be included. The room should be free from obstructions, and should be well lighted and ventilated. The floor should be wooden and if possible covered with an inch of beaver board over which a heavy canvas covering should be drawn. The posts of the ring should be at least eighteen inches outside the ring, and preferably padded. The ropes should be an inch in diameter and wrapped so as to prevent rope burns. The heavy bag should be attached with a short heavy chain to prevent too much swing. The mats and pulleys should be out of the way and not where they will interfere with the boxers.

Hand protection—The human hand was not made for striking. It was made for grasping. It is therefore important to know the correct method of hitting if hand injury is to be prevented. Many hand injuries may be prevented through wrapping or bandaging the hands.

Hand wrapping is an art. It is based upon knowledge of hand anatomy. The hand consists of twenty-seven bones, fourteen bones forming the fingers and thumb, and called phalanges. The five bones forming the back of the hand are called metacarpal bones. The eight wrist bones are the carpal bones. The whole idea of bandaging is to prevent the bones of the hand from spreading, to protect the big knuckle of the thumb, and to support the wrist.

Injury may result from improper bandaging of the hand, so unless the hand is wrapped correctly, it is better to leave it unwrapped.

The best protection for the hand is obtained by using a ten-yard roll of two-inch gauze.

The bandage must not shut off circulation. Have the boxer close the hand several times while bandaging. Never bandage through the fingers, as this spreads the bones and thus defeats the whole purpose of the bandage.

[1] *Ibid.,* p. 35.

For training purposes, canvas or felt bandages may be obtained at any athletic supply house. They can be used constantly and are more economical than gauze bandage.

In punching the light bag, light gloves should be worn to prevent skinning the knuckles. Heavy training gloves should be worn while punching the heavy bag.

Gloves—Heavy fourteen-ounce gloves should be used for all training purposes. The kind with an elastic band at the wrist is preferable to those with laces. They facilitate administration and eliminate a common cause of eye injury.

If gloves with laces are used, instead of tying at the wrist, have the students place the laces in the palms of the hands and hold inside of the gloves. Cut off all metal tips.

Gloves should be cleaned each time after using. Use a damp cloth and saddle soap. Then hang them up to dry.

Watch carefully for rips and tears in the glove, or a bunching and breaking of the padding. Discard such gloves immediately.

Special gloves should be furnished for the heavy bag, and light gloves for the light bag.

Teeth and lip protection—The most frequent injuries are chipped teeth and cut lips. Using a rubber mouthpiece will prevent the majority of such injuries. Insist that each student purchase and use one. They may be obtained at a nominal price from any sporting goods store.

Placing vaseline between the lips and teeth, both upper and lower jaw, helps to prevent injury.

Ear and eye protection—Both are open to injury. Such injuries can be prevented by head helmets which cover the ears completely and which come well down over the forehead. If such a helmet is used the ear and eye injuries will materially decrease.

Protection of the scrotum—Aluminum protection cups should be worn at all times. A deflected blow, an accidentally raised knee are the hazards that are thus eliminated.

The feet—Well-fitting, soft-soled shoes should be worn. Movement is facilitated and slipping prevented. Use plenty of resin and keep water off the floor or canvas. White wool socks should be worn.

Leadership—The most important consideration in the prevention of injuries is adequate leadership. Without leadership facilities and equipment are meaningless.

Instruction—The instructor should be able to teach at least the minimum fundamentals of boxing. Unless an instructor has a basic knowledge of fundamental skills, boxing should not be allowed. An instructor should allow only those who have instruction in fundamentals to box.

Conditioning—An instructor should make sure that every boy who participates in boxing is in good physical condition. The first requisite should be a medical examination, with a permit for every participant on file in the office. This can be either a regular examination or a special one. No boy who has not passed a medical examination should be allowed to box. A medical permit means that the body is organically sound. Besides this an instruction and conditioning program should be followed until the boy is physically able to sustain effort and resist fatigue.

Supervision—Every instructor worthy of the name is careful to supervise any activity in which hazard is present. Boxing, like any other sport, causes no trouble if properly supervised. Only when boxing is carried on without supervision is difficulty encountered.

The officials—Each boy who enters athletic competition is entitled to competent officiating. This is not always the case in boxing. Anyone who is willing to officiate seems to be chosen. This is unfair to the boys. Officials should be selected not only for their knowledge of boxing technique and rules, but for their knowledge and understanding of boys.

The referee

1. Must be a man considerate, sympathetic, and interested in boys. A good sense of humor is important.
2. Must have the ability to control himself at all times if he is to have control of the ring.
3. Must know his own powers. He should execute his full powers but never exceed them.
4. Should know the history of boxing, the development of the rules, and the particular rules under which he is officiating. His knowledge of rules should include amateur, intercollegiate, and professional. (Professional rules vary in each state.)
5. Should abide by the rules at all times and not make up the rules.
6. Should know who is winning at all times and be ready to give his decision instantly.
7. Must be impartial, but firm in his decision.

8. Must keep his hands off the boxers and his only words to the contestants should be "fight," "stop," and "break."
9. Must know when to stop a bout and should always stop it too soon, rather than too late.
10. Should check on the ring and ring equipment before the start of the matches. He should ascertain if all other officials are ready.
11. Must not officiate more than ten bouts at one time. To do so means impairment of judgment.
12. Should have a working knowledge of first-aid.

The judges
1. Should know the skills and techniques of boxing.
2. Should know the rules and the infractions of the rules.
3. Should be familiar with the technique of scoring a bout.
4. Should add up the score at the end of each round.
5. Should not be influenced by the crowd or by last-round rallies.
6. Should not judge more than fifteen consecutive bouts.

The timekeeper
1. Must keep one eye on the bout and one eye on the watch.
2. Should be ready to pick up the count on any knockdowns.

The seconds
1. Should know boxing in all its various phases.
2. Should be sympathetic in nature.
3. Should have a working knowledge of first-aid and a kit consisting of:
   a. water pail, with hand sponge—to clean boxer.
   b. chopped ice and ice water—to stimulate circulation.
   c. water bottle—to rinse mouth.
   d. towels—to wipe and dry boxer.
   e. smelling salts—to clear the head.
   f. stop watch—to time the rounds.
   g. aromatic spirits of ammonia—to settle the stomach.
   h. adrenalin chloride $\frac{1}{1000}$ solution—to stop bleeding.
   i. collodion—to place over old cuts.
   j. swab sticks—to clean a cut or plug the nose.
   k. surgical scissors—to cut tape or bandage.

4. Should stay on the outside of the ring with only his head through. They should be ready to help the boxer when he comes back to the corner. First, try to relax the boxer on the stool. Place his hands in his lap. Wipe him off with a dry towel, using water only if necessary. Don't give him any water to drink unless he asks for it. Have him breathe deeply. Don't talk to the boxer until the last twenty seconds. Then give simple but specific instructions. Keep the voice low and emphasize one thing. Keep repeating the instructions until the bell rings. Then help him off the stool. At the end of the last round wipe the boy off, and help him put on his robe.

IV. FIRST AID TREATMENT OF INJURIES [1, 2, 3]

It is very essential for the boxer, trainer or instructor to know what injuries are most likely to occur and how to administer first-aid when necessary.

STIFFNESS

Results from severe and prolonged exercise which causes fatigue products to accumulate in the blood. To relieve stiffness, take a warm tub bath with the water about 90 degrees Fahrenheit. Place from three to five pounds of epsom salts in the tub. Soak for twenty minutes. A light massage is also good to relieve sore muscles.

SPRAINS

Of the thumb—are caused by blows to the end or side of the thumb. Usually there is some swelling and a dull aching pain which is caused by the ruptured capillaries and the torn ligaments, which in turn cause a small hemorrhage. First stop the effusion. Apply a compression bandage. Then apply ice or cold applications. As soon as effusion is stopped, apply heat—dry, moist, or diathermal. The thumb should then be protected against further injury by bandaging. Continue heat and massage until healed.

Of the shoulder or subdeltoid bursae—Usually caused by trauma or

[1] Lloyd, *op. cit.*, pp. 213-330.
[2] Samuel Bilik, *The Trainers' Bible*. New York: Athletic Trainers Supply Company, 1928, pp. 17-212.
[3] Meanwell, *op. cit.*, pp. 39-154.

strain of the subacromical bursae.[1] The pain is usually found in the left shoulder and is the gnawing kind which seems to burrow right into the bone. Pain is increased with movement. Treatment consists of heat, massage, and passive exercise.

DISLOCATIONS

Of the thumb—may result from boxing contest. Ligaments are injured, nerves torn and capillaries ruptured. There is usually some deformity, pain, and swelling. Grasp the thumb with the right hand and pull, pressing the dislocated bone back into place with the left hand. Then treat as a sprain. Place in cold water or cover with ice packs. The next day apply heat and massage. Then bandage. Start bending the joint the second day to prevent adhesions. Continue until normality is regained.

WOUNDS

Eyecuts—are very common boxing injuries, and are due to blows on the eyebrows. Apply a few drops of $\frac{1}{1000}$ solution of adrenalin chloride with an eye dropper to stop bleeding. Monsel powder or iron chloride will coagulate blood but should be used only by expert handlers. As soon as possible refer the boxer to a physician.

Split lip—is caused by a blow on the lip which forces the soft tissue against the teeth. Saturate a pad of cotton in adrenalin and place it next to the cut. Pressure of the lip on the gum will stop the bleeding. Watch closely for infection and if the cut is deep, send the boxer to a physician.

Bruises and abrasions—are caused by blows which remove the top layer of skin and which to some degree damage underlying tissues. Wash well with soap and water. Then apply a non-irritating antiseptic. Cover with a sterile pad.

A broken tooth—Unless a mouth-piece is used, a straight blow to the mouth will often break, chip or crack the front teeth. If this happens, refer the boys to a dentist.

Nosebleed—is caused by a direct blow on the nose which ruptures some of the small capillaries in the septum. Do not allow the nose to be blown. Try to contract the blood vessels by use of cold applications or apply a piece of ice under the upper lip. Pinching or compressing

[1] Bursae are sacs or pads which facilitate movement between contiguous structures.

the nostrils together for a few moments often succeeds in stopping the hemorrhage. If quick action is necessary, place a swab stick saturated in adrenalin, up the nose.

A broken nose—is indicated by a history of trauma, soreness, swelling, movement and internal hemorrhage. Have the boxer report to a nose specialist at once so that no deformity or nasal obstruction results.

The black eye—is the badge of the pugilist. It is caused by a blow on the eye which ruptures the small capillaries, thus causing hemorrhage into the surrounding tissue. As bleeding stops, the blood decomposes causing the different shades of discoloration. Apply a piece of ice directly to the eye. When the swelling has stopped, heat is applied, usually by hot packs. Later, the next day, a light circular massage may be used along with heat applications.

A thumb in the eye—often occurs during a bout. Extreme irritation is caused and the eye constantly waters. Hemorrhage often results. Apply cold applications to stop hemorrhage. Send the boxer to an oculist as soon as possible.

The "cauliflower" ear—is the badge of both the boxing and wrestling professions. It is also referred to as a "tin ear." It indicates a lack of proper attention as a "cauliflower" ear is unnecessary. It is the result of a blow on the ear which causes a rupture of the small capillaries into the fatty tissue of the ear forming a blood tumor. The tumor shuts off nutrition between the cartilage and the overlying tissue causing decomposition. The blood coagulates, hardens and becomes organized into connective tissue. A shrinking takes place obliterating all regular ear markings, leaving a crinkled mass known as a "cauliflower" ear.

Hemorrhage should be stopped as soon as possible. Use ice packs with pressure. If bleeding continues take the boxer to a physician and have the blood drawn out by means of a hypodermic syringe. However, unless a compress bandage is used, it will fill up again. To prevent this [1]

> Take a piece of cotton which is large enough to fill the cavity where the injury is located, and soak in collodion. Mold the saturated cotton to the cavity of the ear and hold in place by strips of adhesive tape. When the ether evaporates the cotton will become hard and act as a splint, and prevent the recurrence of the hemorrhage.

[1] Lloyd, *op. cit.*, p. 279.

If this fails, have the doctor make a small cross incision in the most congested part. Then place in the incision a small strip of sterilized gauze to serve as a drain.

The broken rib—is indicated by pain when breathing, a sharp pain when lifting the arms, or tenderness in the rib area. Have the injury cared for by a physician. The immobilization by binding with tape is the prescribed treatment.

THE KNOCKOUT BLOW TO THE CHIN

The "point" of the chin has long been a target for boxers. The jaw-bone acts as a lever and a blow to the end of the chin relays the force almost directly to the medulla. As the medulla controls the cardiac-respiratory mechanism, paralysis and unconsciousness result. A terrific blow direct to the "point" may be enough to jar the cerebral hemispheres and produces a mild concussion.

To restore consciousness, apply restoratives, twist and pull the ears, rub the neck, chafe the hands, pat the face, pull the arms and legs and apply ice to the spine. When consciousness is regained, find out if the boy knows his own name. Obtain medical attention as soon as possible. After medical aid, wrap the individual in warm blankets and give him some hot tea.

THE SOLAR PLEXUS KNOCKOUT

The solar plexus was known as Broughton's mark in the early days of the prize ring. It was not until after Corbett's defeat at Carson City that the blow became known as the solar plexus blow.

The solar plexus is situated above the middle line of the upper border of the pancreas just opposite the margin of the diaphragm. It is a large collection of nerve cells and forms the great center of the sympathetic nervous system. It is attached to the second and third sacral nerves. A blow to the solar plexus affects the vagus nerve causing a reflex which inhibits or depresses both the cardiac and respiratory mechanism.[1] "The heart is invariably slowed and weakened, respiration becomes gasping and paroxysmal in type, pulse thready, eyes starey and glassy, and the whole vitality lowered." [2]

Such a picture is one of shock and first-aid should be given for shock. Apply smelling salts. Cold water applied to the back of the

[1] Lewis, *op. cit.*, p. 223.
[2] *Loc. cit.*

neck is effective. Loosen all constrictions. When breathing is resumed, place the individual under the observation of a physician. Place the feet higher than the head. Place a blanket over the patient and insist on a twenty- or thirty-minute rest.

"DEMENTIA PUGILISTICA"

Often referred to as just plain "punch drunk." It is a condition caused by too many severe beatings about the head. It is a comparatively rare condition and not common to amateur or intercollegiate boxing.

Physiologically, it is possible that the constant jar of blows may cause small hemorrhages in the brain. The blood thus liberated is eventually organized into connective tissue, shutting off the blood supply to the brain cells involved, causing their death. Once gone brain tissue cannot be replaced.

What can be done? In the first place it is believed that only certain types can ever become "punch drunk." Some persons are so constructed that no amount of beatings on the head will cause hemorrhage, while others can stand only moderate punishment before hemorrhage will result. Boxing alone does not cause this condition. Any activity which causes constant jar to the head can cause this condition to result. Diving and football are two other sports which subject the head to constant jar and injury.

Persons who seem to be easily hurt, who suffer a headache after a boxing match, after diving, or a football game, should turn their athletic activity to sports in which physical contact does not enter.

It is the responsibility of leadership in boxing to make sure that people susceptible to head injuries do not participate. Leadership in boxing must prevent any boy from taking a severe beating. Correct instruction and good officiating should help take care of this point.

Dementia pugilistica or "punch drunkenness," a rare condition that can happen, should and can be entirely eliminated from the sport of boxing.

INDEX

— Notes —

— Notes —

— Notes —

— Notes —